PARENTING FOR AGES 3 TO 8

THE
FAMILY COACH
METHOD

RAISING GOOD, KIND, ETHICAL KIDS

IN A COMPLICATED WORLD

PARENTING FOR AGES 3 TO 8

THE
FAMILY COACH
METHOD

RAISING GOOD, KIND, ETHICAL KIDS

IN A COMPLICATED WORLD

Dr. Lynne Kenney

st. lynn's
press

PITTSBURGH

The Family Coach Method
Raising Good, Kind, Ethical Kids in a Complicated World

ISBN-13: 978-0-9819615-0-7

Library of Congress Control Number: 2009924725
CIP information available upon request

First Edition, 2009

St. Lynn's Press . POB 18680 . Pittsburgh, PA 15236
412.466.0790 . www.stlynnspress.com

Typesetting – Holly Wensel, Network Printing Services
Cover design – Jeff Nicoll
Editors – Catherine Dees, Abby Dees

Cover Photo – Joe and Alexandra DeHaven

Note to the reader:
In writing about client cases, the author has changed the names of actual people, as well as other identifying statements about them, out of respect for their privacy. Special, loving thanks to Susan Link for her drawing on page 139. And to Olivia and Allie Markan, ages 10 and 9, for their drawings on pages xv and 75.

Printed in the United States of America
on recycled paper ♲

This title and all of St. Lynn's Press books may be purchased for educational, business, or sales promotional use. For information please write: Special Markets Department . St. Lynn's Press POB 18680 . Pittsburgh, PA 15236

10 9 8 7 6 5 4 3 2 1

Dedication

With gratitude I dedicate *The Family Coach Method*
to my parents, my brothers, my husband and children.
We live and love as a village. I adore you.

TABLE OF CONTENTS

I

Create a Foundation of Values

II

Teach Your Children Skills Within the Context of Your Relationship

III

Manage Behaviors With Freedom and Consequenceland

❧

INTRODUCTION

❧

My Promise To You

Your experience reading this book will be different from your past experiences with parenting books. Even if you have "tried it all before," by the time you get to Chapter 3 your family is going to be different. Your parenting experiences are going to be marked by peace and joy. Your children are going to have a better grasp of what you expect of them and how to do as expected. How can I say this... and why is it worth your time to embark on this journey with me? Because I'm confident that I can help any family (and I mean *any*) to be happier, more balanced and more of a winning team, instead of pulling in all different directions and getting nowhere fast. I've done this with hundreds of families and I can help you do it with yours. I'm going to help you create Your Extraordinary Family. That's my promise.

❧

Let's begin with the fact that you are already a great parent. You are full of insights, strategies and ideas on how to help your children explore, learn and grow. You have images of who your children will become and how you will help them get there.

But perhaps, some days, you feel something is missing. There may be times when you aren't quite sure how to respond to your child. Your son refuses to buckle his car seat, you encourage, then cajole, then perhaps threaten. You find yourself feeling powerless. Your children refuse to complete their morning chores, they throw food at the dinner table or melt down when it's time to turn off the TV. In those times, parenting can feel more like a frustrating battle of wills than a joyful time of watching your children grow. We've all been there.

The sad fact is that most parenting strategies today are seat-of-the-pants affairs invoked "in the moment," which too often means mismanagement and punishment, rather than teaching and skill development.

Each week I speak with intelligent, experienced parents like you. Time and again, they tell me they are looking for an approach to parenting that helps their children thrive and succeed as loving, caring beings. They've tried their best, but something has been missing: a *method* – a specific approach to what you do as a parent and how you do it. Enter The Family Coach Method.

The Family Coach Method is built upon proactive prevention strategies, putting your relationship with your children back at the center of your parenting, and limiting the amount of time you have to spend managing your children with punishment.

As you may have already noticed, punishment as a parenting method is usually unsuccessful. But parenting with a defined family culture, in a family that is dedicated to kindness and cooperation, works. The key is collaborative strategies designed to increase your child's buy-in to the family life you prescribe.

What makes The Method unique is its emphasis on teaching proactive behavioral expectations and cooperation strategies within a secure parental relationship. If you have been living in damage control mode and applying discipline and consequences only after rule violations have occurred, let me ask you: How has that been working for you? I think we both know the answer.

Grow You, Grow Your Child

We're going to be talking about your children, but first, let's take a moment and talk about you. You're a bright parent, a parent who is interested in raising the healthiest children possible. You may read books, explore blogs and communicate with your children's teachers about how they are doing in school.

You may wonder, "What else do I need to know and understand in order to be the best parent I can be?"

I suggest that if you know these five things, you are well on your way:

1. **The developmental abilities of your child at different ages and stages**

2. **How to provide your child with opportunities to develop "next step" skills as they grow**

3. **How to identify the difference between a skill deficit and willful non-compliance**

4. **How to reinforce and reward positive behaviors**

5. **How to shape your child's behavior as a foundation of a loving parent-child relationship**

As you work with each of these areas, you are going to notice something else happening, as well. Many times, we'll be talking about your children, but we're also talking about you. We all have a piece in the puzzle of family life. Being prepared to make changes in your own words, actions, tone and demeanor will set you apart from the parents who continue wishing desperately for their children to change, yet they are unwilling to do so themselves.

The Family Coach Method teaches you the skills, strategies and solutions to communicate an expected behavior, evaluate whether or not your child possesses the skill set to exhibit that behavior, and then encourage your child's success with love, warmth and tenderness.

Parents Like You

Most of the families I work with are intelligent, competent and appealing. Some are even hysterically funny, which I adore. Each and every one of them is invested in raising happy children. When parents tell me, "My child does not do as he is told," that is my opening. *Yes,* I think, *now we're talkin'.*

What parents initially want to learn is, "How do I discipline my child properly?" Fair enough, but what they really need to be asking is "How do I teach my child?" That is the crux of The Family Coach Method. When a child exhibits a rule violation, he is asking to be taught, mentored and guided. That, parents, is the hard work. The good new is, you have everything to gain and not a thing to lose.

It starts with defining the culture you want your children to grow and thrive in. You may feel there's not a great deal you can do about changing the larger culture of society, but you are a powerful force in defining a culture for your own family.

The Journey

Many of us plan for the baby shower. We think about bringing baby home and what we'll choose for the baby layette. We plan and plan for birthing our babies. But very few of us think about how we're going to raise our children over a lifetime. We take life partners, have our children, and then just when our children are old enough to begin developing their sense of independence, around age 2, we begin to wonder...what do we do now?

The challenge is that as bright parents we raise our babies quite well until about age 24-36 months, when they start to become independent beings – and then we are not sure how to guide, mentor and teach.

We're here today to find out. In *The Family Coach Method* we're going to explore concepts, ideas and strategies that may be new to you. Before I had children they were new to me too. That's where this journey began, in my own parenting experience, and that's what led me to do what I do today: rug-level, step-by-step teaching so that we can all become not just great parents, but expert parents.

How I Realized Every Parent Needs a Primer on How to Raise Good Kids

Over the past two decades, I have had the pleasure of interacting with parents who wish to create a better life for their children and themselves. Usually, this entails a process of listing problems and solutions that the family can practice both in my office and at their home. Many families come to me because their children are having difficulty in school, not developing the socialization skills to be good rule-followers or refusing to do as they are told at home.

Some families have children with symptoms on the ADHD or anxiety spectrums, so sensory meltdowns, separation anxiety, and oppositionalism are a big challenge. Since many of the families I meet have children who experience problems with organization, planning and impulse control, I have learned, over time, that The Family Coach Method is beneficial for these children and families as well.

Fifteen years ago when I was working as a pediatric psychologist, a family would come to my office and I would often see them for 20 weeks, fully reimbursed by insurance. We could spend a lot of time in needs assessment, planning and treatment. But as the health industry changed, insurance reimbursements diminished and soon families began to need a "faster fix" for unhealthy habits that had taken a few years to develop. Now they were most often paying out of pocket for our work, so being efficient and effective became a top priority.

I quickly learned that the most efficient and effective thing I could do was to actually visit the landscape where the challenges lived. So I started meeting families in their homes, on playgrounds, on tennis courts and in classrooms.

Before I studied pediatric psychology, I earned a master's degree in Physical Education with a specialization in Sport Psychology. Through my training and in-the-trenches experience, I realized that it is possible to get right to the heart of building a better family in a matter of *hours*, not months, using strategies I had employed with athletes in the past. I began to apply proactive skill development to parenting – with amazing results.

I saw change come quickly and powerfully, using a 1-2-3 approach:

1. **Data Collection** *(honing parental observation skills)*
2. **Decision Making**
3. **Implementation**

As The Family Coach Method evolved, I soon found that we were generating great solutions to common parenting problems, in a systematic, thoughtful manner. Being invited into parents' homes or into school classrooms, I would apply the proactive, positive strategies of The Method, and the changes would be immediate and dramatic. No longer was the focus on diagnosis or pathology. The spotlight was now on health and wellness. Parents could become their own skilled Family Coaches. Teachers could apply the concepts in their classrooms. My job was simply to give them the tools to do it.

Visualizing The Method

The Family Coach Method is both linear and circular. It is firm but flexible; it is a new way of living that is steeped in developing secure relationships with your children, with clear expectations, collaborative agreements and a well defined culture in which you and your family agree to live.

The Method is step-by-step. That's the linear part. We begin by laying a firm foundation of values upon which you build a family mission and well defined rules for positive behaviors in your family. Then we move to the actual words and actions you take to reinforce the cultural expectations of your family. Finally, we explore what to do when your children do not live as they have agreed to within your family culture. In each part of The Method there is a clearly defined beginning, middle and end.

These expectations and behaviors also build on themselves. Mastery of one skill and behavior opens the door to a new life challenge, a new expectation within the family culture, and the development of that new skill, and so on, and so on. In this way, the Family Coach

Method is also circular: You clarify an expectation for your children, they use the skills to cooperate with that expectation and you reinforce and reward their accomplishments with love, attention, warmth, clear communication and happy moments in your relationships...and the cycle continues.

*　*　*

Most families don't have the income to spend a thousand dollars or more on counseling for parenting issues, so I reassigned the role of the parent from "client" to "expert." I began developing written tools that parents could use in their homes to achieve their extraordinary family lives, with a bit of guided teaching, consultation and caring.

I wanted them to take advantage of an overarching concept I call Better Family Living, which is the entirety of the behavioral, developmental, learning and nutritional interventions that help a family to thrive, with peaceful interactions and skillful behaviors.

Really, when it comes down to it, if a parent will invest a few minutes a day in developing and implementing a plan, using The Method as a template, a family can be transformed in 90 days or less. Sometimes it only takes a week!

We're in this together

As we move forward on this parenting journey we'll explore the world of your child. We'll talk about what it means to be 3 to 8 years of age. We'll review the importance of a firm foundation of values as a defining feature of creating Your Extraordinary Family. Most of all, we will focus on helping your children succeed by giving them the skills they need to discover, explore and grow.

Before I begin many of the talks I so happily participate in with parents, I say, "You know that family in the superstore last week, with the tantruming kids? That was my family." We all laugh...been there, definitely done that.

I'm not even embarrassed to say it, 'cause I'm in this with you, in the world we call parenting. Tantrums in supermarkets and stores big enough to hold two football games at once are common places for losing control. It's actually pretty normal. These places are over-stimulating to children, with all their tempting chemical treats, loud noises and bright lights.

Worry-not if your children melt down, refuse your demands and argue with one another. Even though your children are healthy and thriving, every child has some challenges. How would we grow without the challenges? We're human. This makes us real and vulnerable. It can also give us strength, kindness and compassion.

As parents, we are real and vulnerable as well. We use our best guesses for how to interact with our children. Many of our interactions are related or similar to how adults interacted with us in the past. Perhaps you were raised in a family guided by a mission, values or a plan. If your parents were experienced teachers or entrepreneurs they might have known about goal setting, creating a vision and planning for the future. If they were free spirits in the 60's and 70's, they might have been less skilled about creating structure, but excellent at encouraging your creativity.

What I have learned in 21 years of interacting with families and living in them myself, is that *we communicate our values to our children every day through our words and our behavior.* What we will do in this book, together, is develop a plan with the structure and guidance to communicate a mutually understood foundation of mission and values to your children. You will be creating your own unique family culture in a collaborative process with your children. This means that what you do from here on out as a parent will have real meaning and purpose. You will move from being reactive to being proactive and mindfully responsive – from being frustrated to feeling at peace.

It is my belief that children wish to behave well. They have an innate desire to be connected, feel loved and be valued. When you begin to *listen, talk* and *share* with your children at eye level, you will be amazed by how quickly your children shift from disobedience to masterful skill fulfillment.

I will be honest: Most families I meet, no matter how educated or intelligent, have usually not thought much about how they are defining their family culture. When I ask questions such as: "What kind of family do you want to raise?" and "How do you communicate those expectations to your children?" they often go blank, as though this is a graduate level math exam. But it isn't. It's basic family management, and it's not hard at all.

In the pages that follow, you will learn how to develop children who...

+ **Know what kind of family they live in**
+ **Know what is expected of them**
+ **Know how to behave thoughtfully**

Even more importantly, you and your children will be able to weather those times when they or you make a mistake or an error in judgment – because your family will be able to rely on that basic foundation of love, compassion and respect that you have built. Together.

Let's dive in!

How To Use This Book

❧

My hope is that you will use this book to help you become your own Family Coach, the parenting expert in your own home.

Your Home As a Picture

In these pages, we are actually going to create a metaphorical home in which you live. My colleague Lori Shulman and I call this approach to defining how you live and why you live that way "Behavioral Architecture." The term refers to the words, written plans and drawings you use to define your family culture, way of life and the behavioral expectations you have for your children.

To begin with, we are going to work together, just as we would if I visited your home. Don't worry, it's all a metaphor – you don't have to go clean up or anything.

In a few moments, we are going to begin drawing out and laying down the foundation of your family culture. You'll design this foundation for and with your children so that they clearly understand the kind of family in which they are being raised. We are going to identify and communicate your family values in a manner that is meaningful to both you and your children. Then we are going to define the rules by which your family lives within this structure. It's going to be fun, energizing and enlightening.

❧

Organization of *The Family Coach Method*

I have divided the book into three sections:

I. Communicate a foundation of values

II. Teach your children skills within the context of your relationship

III. Manage behaviors with Freedom and Consequenceland

What's Inside

+ Each section and chapter is sequential, with **signposts, questions, exercises** and **activities** designed to take you step-by-step, from a family that may be in turmoil to one of peace and happiness.

+ You will find **behavior examples, case studies** and **situation scenarios**, with lots of sample dialogue to show you how you can take a similar situation in your own family and bring it to a positive outcome.

+ Here and there, I've sprinkled tasty **How I Do It** items, which offer my own parenting experiences. You'll also discover many enlightening "How I Do It's" from well-known names in the expert mom and nanny world – like Kathy Ireland, designer and author of *Real Solutions for Busy Moms*, and Michelle LaRowe, nanny extraordinaire and author of the parenting series, *Nanny to the Rescue!*

+ **The Family Coach Toolbox:** In many places I will call out and explain a particularly useful tool for your family's parenting Toolbox (look for the Toolbox icon).

+ **Activities:** Throughout the book I present collaborative activities for your family, designed to develop your children's skills as well as your own. If you are like me, a visual person who needs to make lists, drawings, diagrams and "mind maps," you may be delighted by and have fun with the activities on these pages. You'll dive into writing things down, posting them up and covering your walls with new words and behaviors that remind you and your children what you expect and how to behave.

✦ **Hands-On with The Family Coach:** At the end of many chapters you will find a dedicated Activities section that builds on the ideas presented in that chapter – some of it serious, some of it fun, and all created to help you identify and affirm what you're about as a family. Of course, I would love it if you tried each and every activity, but even if you don't, just take the opportunity to reflect on them and share your thoughts with your family.

✦ **The Family Coach Playbook:** You might find it helpful to make your very own Playbook. As a companion to *The Family Coach Method* this could be something you'll find yourself referring to every day (see Chapter 1, Activity #1 for how to create your Playbook). You can use your Playbook to write, draw and scribble your way to your newly defined family. As you find comments, pages, tips and activities in this book that appeal to you, copy them and put them in your Playbook. Make notations, cut, paste and doodle to your heart's desire. This will be your book to create, so do with it as you like. (How many authors say "copy my book"? I do, go for it!)

It's all valuable. I wouldn't promise you Your Extraordinary Family without giving you lots of terrific tools to work with!

I strongly encourage you to start at the beginning and move through each chapter in sequence. As you've heard me say already (and you will again), many parents I work with wish to jump straight to discipline. This is understandable, especially if they feel over-whelmed by what's going on at home. We're taught to think that punishment is the most powerful tool, but it isn't. Yes, I will address discipline at length in the last chapter, but please believe me, the best starting point is developing a secure relationship with your chil-dren. Once you clarify the kind of family you wish to be, communi-cate your expectations clearly to your children and reinforce positive behaviors in your family, you will seldom need punishment.

One More Thing...

Whether you enjoy this book in a relaxed manner on a plane or you sit with it at your dining room table, writing and drawing plans for the family you dream of becoming, you have the power and freedom to use this book as you desire. These are my concepts, but this is your family. You create it, design it and lead it.

I

CREATE A FOUNDATION OF VALUES

Olivia

CHAPTER 1

THE FOUNDATION

If I were invited to your home we'd begin at rug level, where the kids are. Maybe we'd find a comfortable place to gather on the floor in the family room, or maybe at the kitchen table. I'd pull out some paper and markers and I'm smiling, because I know that we're starting a journey of discovery together. This work is a pleasure for me; it's energizing. You might be a little anxious at first, worried I'd pass judgment or notice that you could be doing things better...but that would quickly fade because, as I'd explain, this parenting thing – we're all in it together. So we'd talk a bit about what's currently going well at home and what could be working better for you.

If the children aren't already present, I might ask if they could join us. I'd ask them about themselves. I'd pass around some paper and we'd all choose our favorite colors of marker or crayons. Then I'd invite them to talk about your family rules.

"This is my first time here," I say to your children. "Can you tell me what your family rules are? I want to make sure I follow your rules."

Almost before the words are out of my mouth I'm hearing:

"You can't eat ice cream before dinner"

"You need to do what Mom and Dad say"

"You can't climb on the furniture..."

What fun! The children are usually so adorable, whether 3 or 8 or in-between. So now I'm getting a sense that this family has rules and has communicated them to the children. I'm hearing mostly *don'ts*, but that's not surprising. Most families are big on don'ts.

We spend a few minutes drawing pictures about the rules, and when I feel the energy starting to ebb, I'll say to one of the children, "I'm going to break a family rule. Can you tell me what I'm doing wrong?" Then I get up, go over to the sofa and start to perch on the back of it.

I hear: *"You're not supposed to do that!"*

Then I go to the pantry and take a cookie, and I hear: *"You can't take cookies without asking!"*

"OK," I say, "I know what I'm *not* supposed to do, but how do I know what am I *supposed* to do? Can you tell me how everybody in your family knows what they're supposed to do?" Puzzled looks.

At this point, it's time for you and me to get down to the real work of the hour: **defining the kind of family you want to raise and deciding what words and actions you'd use to explain your family culture – your *do's* – to your children.** With grown-up talk starting, the kids run off to play. It's amazing how even a 3- and 4-year-old can get busy with play dough or drawing or a movie, knowing that their parents are designing a happier family. You might not think they know, but trust me, they do.

Every family has a culture of its own

Your family has a special culture, defined by you, your history, your dreams and aspirations. Understanding what your family culture is and how you wish to communicate it to your children is part of the magic in The Family Coach Method. We so rarely think about how we live, why we do as we do, and why we wish for our children to be as we desire. If all you do with this book is reflect on your family culture – how, what, when, where and why you do what you do as a family – and communicate that culture to your children, I will be a happy author and mom.

Your first concrete step as a parent is to establish a firm foundation for your children. This means communicating a clear foundation of behavioral expectations.

Every family needs a foundation

If you are raising a child between the ages of 3 and 8, you are raising a child who is in the midst of defining who he is and figuring out how to be the most skillful child possible. Your child learns from you all about the playing field of life. He is developing the language and social skills to move from the comfort and care of home to the social world of school-aged children. These are among the most important aspects of your child's development between 3 and 8, and you as a parent are here to see that your child has the best possible foundation on which to live, grow, develop and thrive.

On this page I've made a line drawing of a house. That's where we're going next. Imagine for a moment that this represents your family home (I'm sure yours has straighter windows!).

Tell me, what is the most important part of it? The roof? The walls? No. The most important part of your home is its foundation. If that isn't laid down securely, your house will be vulnerable to all kinds of stresses; it could even fall down around your ears. The same is true of parenting. Your family's foundation is the solid structure that supports it through good times and bad, no matter what's going on in the world outside. It represents your reason for being, what you stand for and the code by which you live each day. It is your bedrock strength as a family.

The Family Coach Method starts with laying down your family's three foundational elements: Mission Statement, Values and Rules – and building up from there. With this in mind, let's look again at my drawing.

Your mission statement is the foundation's floor – what you stand for and stand on. Rising out of that are the two strong support pillars of your values and your rules. If thoughtfully implemented, these three foundational elements allow you to build the extraordinary family that can be yours.

Your Extraordinary Family
The Who, the What, and the How

The *Who* is your Mission Statement. This is a continuing reminder to you and your children of who you are as a family unit *("We are a family who...")*.

The *What* are your Values. What you value shows you the way to your family's goals. It propels your mission *("As a family we value...")*.

The *How* are your Rules. Rules are the "how we do it." They are the building blocks for expected behaviors – your family's *do's* (and a few *don'ts*). Rules implement your values and set up the secure framework for you and your children *("We do X because it supports our mission and values...")*.

With these three elements securely in place, you have the best chance of weathering difficulties that might otherwise be overwhelming. That's promising a lot, but in my years of working with families in all kinds of situations, I know it to be true. So, let's explore your family's foundation and get you started.

Your Mission Statement

What is a Mission Statement?

In recent years many businesses and organizations have begun writing mission statements to define themselves, their ethics and aspirations, to their employees and clients. Far more than a wish list, it is a statement of what truly matters, of goals and principles, among other things. It can be brief or complex, but it usually sets out the standards under which the entity intends to operate. My husband's business, for example, has a mission statement that sits on the reception desk for all to see. I see it every time I come to his office and I am reminded each time of the high ethical standards that he adheres to in his work.

So, how would I present this concept to your family if I were visiting for the first time? We grown-ups might sit together at the kitchen table or in the playroom and I'd ask you to tell me something about the family you were raised in. What did it stand for? What messages were communicated to you about what you did, how you did it and why you did it? Would you say that you were raised with a family mission, even if it was unwritten or undefined? Looking back, did your parents have expectations for you and your behavior?

After some discussion I would ask you to tell me about the expectations you have for your own children. It's not always going to be a free-flowing conversation at first, because it may be difficult to put those expectations into words – which tells me that you, as a caring, well-meaning parent have not yet been able to clearly communicate what your expectations are to your children, and why you have those expectations. When that kind of clear communication is lacking, parents will often move straight to discipline in order to achieve compliance. In my experience as a pediatric psychologist and The Family Coach, that's not the proper place to start if you want a successful, happy family. But please know that I absolutely *do* understand the stresses of trying to be an "everything" parent, and those moments of utter despair when a child is defiant or out of control. We're going to find solutions together.

5

Are you a family with a mission?

Let's step all the way back to what kind of family you want to raise and why this is important to you. First, some questions to get your thoughts flowing:

✦ Do you want to raise children who are respectful?

✦ Do you want to raise children who value their education?

✦ Do you want to live in a happy home?

✦ Do you want to live in a peaceful home?

✦ Do you want to live in a home where family members feel loved?

✦ Do you want to live in an organized home?

Now let's go a little deeper. Since so much of parenting involves just taking care of what's happening today – getting everyone dressed and off to school, making sure the shoes are on the right feet and starting your own day – there's seldom space in our lives to take a deep breath and think about the big picture...what we're here for, where we're going together. So I'm going to ask you some of those longer-range questions right now. They are meant to help focus your thoughts and reveal to you what's most important to your unique family. You might be surprised at what you discover. Here goes:

✦ Why do you exist? (That's a biggie. How do you envision your purpose as an individual and as a parent?)

✦ What's really important to you?

✦ Twenty years from now, what are you hoping that your children will say about you?

✦ What will they learn about life from you?

✦ Who do you want your children to become?

✦ What kind of parent can you become?

✦ What are you willing to do to create a peaceful, loving home?

✦ Are you ready to learn a new way of being, based in love?

The answers don't have to come quickly. This is a process that can't be forced or rushed. An answer may come to you in the middle of the night with an aha! Or something your child says to you in the car will lead to a small revelation. However the answers come, it's because you have asked the right questions. You're starting to think of the big picture for yourself and your family. *You will know you are really in the flow when your revelations take you beyond the aha! to a new feeling or behavior – a new way of being and loving.*

Now you can go back to that first list of questions above and think again about the kind of family you want to raise. Most of us will answer Yes to all of them. It all comes down to happiness, doesn't it? We want happy children and a loving family. That's not too much to ask. But it's up to you to take the steps to make it so.

The first step is identifying your family's mission and having the children take part. And then, when everyone has had a chance to contribute, it will be time to put your new mission statement into writing – making it a tangible reminder that you are a unified team, all on the same playing field.

For now, I want you to be comfortable with the whole idea, so I'm going to help you come to the point of actually knowing who you are as a family and what your mission is. (I will be doing this for each of the three foundational steps – Mission, Values and Rules.)

Thinking About Your Family Mission:
"We are a family who…"

Your mission is about your family, it's aspirational, it describes the kind of family you wish to be. A mission statement is a guiding light, a symbol of where you want to aim your family over a lifetime. But it is not meant to be carved in stone, forever and ever the same. So you shouldn't be too concerned about creating a "document for the ages." It may change as your children grow; it can be flexible and shift with you over time.

Your Mission is a statement that you will come back to now and again as you parent your children. For example, once your mission is a reality, you may find yourself referring to it to remind your children why certain behaviors are not "who we are as a family." That can be very powerful.

Let's begin with getting a clear definition of what kind of family you are. When you sit as a family at the dinner table or you walk to school, you might talk about what it means to be a family with a mission. Let your children know "we're all going to think about what kind of family we want to be." You might help them by explaining that having a mission means creating a space in which we live our values and our family rules. You could prompt their thinking by asking, "Are we the kind of family who cares for one another?"... "Are we are the kind of family who welcomes friends and family into our home?" "What kind of family do we want to be?"

There is no one-size-fits-all family, and no one-size-fits-all mission statement

Families respond to the development of a family mission differently I have worked with families who write one overall mission for the family and then one aspirational goal or mission for each child. Each child is special in his or her own way, and their mission statements will show this: One child may aspire to be a great athlete, another child may seek to be a good friend to animals. For you and your child, this is your own unique mission statement and you can create it the way that is most meaningful to you. It might be one sentence or a paragraph. It might be simple or elaborate. *It is yours.*

Here are a few examples, some long, some short, written by real families like yours:

"The mission of our family is to provide a home environment that encourages honesty, fairness, respect and love. We work together to ensure that each member of our family feels important and has the support and the tools they need to reach their higher goals."

"We reach out to others to promote respect for all people in our daily life."

"We are a family that regards education as the foundation of success. Having reached our educational goals, we will give back to others in order to share our success."

"We are a family who has fun. We live for joy and spending time together."

There is no right or wrong way to do this, as you can see. But one thing is consistently true of the families I have worked with: **Your values drive your mission.**

How you perceive your life and what you really care about is an expression of your values. Remember the drawing of our imaginary house? The three foundational elements must *all* work together to make your home solid and strong. So let's talk about the values pillar of your foundation as you prepare to create your mission statement.

YOUR VALUES

Defining Your Values

Whether conservative or liberal, religious or agnostic, multi-cultural or uni-cultural, you have values that you live by every day. Your values may be about showing others that you are a success, or your values may be about "lifting one another up." Your behavior is the outside representation of what you value. If you wonder about what you value, look at your daily behavior and actions. Do you get up in the morning and do yoga? Do you enjoy making breakfast and eating as a family before you start your day? Do you have a family game night? Do you attend services every week? All of these activities reflect what you care about, what matters to you. These reflect what you value. If you work hard, you value hard work; if you play hard, you value play. Maybe both values apply, or entirely different ones.

Simply look at what you do and how you live. Talk with your partner about what he or she values; ask your friends what they value. Notice how people exhibit their own values in the world around you. You might find yourself starting to take notes or making lists. That can be very helpful. I never find myself without a notepad and pen, just in case something comes into my head that I don't want to lose!

What Really Matters: *"As a Family, we value . . ."*

If I were visiting with your family, we'd explore the idea of values. I might ask your children, "What really matters to you? "... "What are some of the most important things to you?" I never know what to expect, but it's always a pleasure to listen to your children. They will say and do the cutest things, so very earnest as they try to respond to my questions. Your three-year-old might run to her room then and scurry back carrying all her prized stuffed animals. They are all welcome, as they represent what your child is attached to. Toy trucks and cars might join us as well. We'd place them on the table and talk about why they matter, why your child values them. An older child, say an 8-year-old, might speak to me about fairness, because his experiences in school have shown him how important that is. These are good conversations to have, as you are starting to show your children the meaning and importance of having values.

Values are more than words

I generally think of values as nouns, often single words that say a lot: integrity, honesty, responsibility, education, athleticism, kindness and respect. I imagine you are teaching your children values each day. What words come to your mind?

Out of a conversation of values, the two I hear most often are **love** and **respect**. On my visit with your family I would discuss the meaning of respect in your home. Your children want us to respect them. They might also like us to respect their prized possessions. On an ongoing basis I would recommend that you talk with your children about what respect means and how it works with your shared values.

Kathy Ireland is an expert mom, talented designer and author of *Real Solutions for Busy Moms*. She is committed to the importance of incorporating her family's values into all parts of their life together. Here is a values-friendly tip that Kathy wants to share with us:

How I Make "Bubble Time" at Home

Children at every age respond to what they see as much as they respond to what they hear. Therefore, when you put your values first, your children's behavior will follow. As an example, in our family, respect is an important value. We show respect for family time in our home with a concept called Bubble Time. This is a special time just for us, together. We ask our kids to put the outside world on hold, and we do as well. No technology or phone calls. This is when we close the doors on the outside world, play games, talk and enjoy one another. These moments make us closer. Bubble Time works for us. I recommend you give it a try. **K.I.**

Values lead to effective discipline

I want to just touch on discipline at this point – we'll go much deeper into discipline and non-compliance later on. But I'd like you to be thinking about the fact that your discipline style is closely connected to your values. Your values are your reference for positive behavioral expectations in your family. Your family values reflect the mission you have established. Your values also reinforce your family rules, the second pillar upon your home's strong foundation.

Once you have identified and confirmed your family values as a whole, then discipline becomes clear, consistent and predictable. You now have specific values you can refer to, which your children will understand and recognize: "We value kindness, so we help our brothers and sisters when they need us."... "We value respect, so we do as Daddy asks the first time."

When you have a situation where children do not live by expected family values, rather than moving directly to punishment or confrontation, really knowing what your values are gives you the tools to guide the situation in a better way. Your goal now is to help your children to develop skills and habits that are *values-based*.

Here are some values-based responses that a parent might offer in the midst of a mini-crisis:

> *"Hey, we said we're a family who respects one another with our words."*
>
> *"Calling your sister stupid doesn't sound respectful."*
>
> *"What's another way you can you tell your sister you are not happy with her behavior?"*
>
> *"Do you want to ask her to do something differently?"*
>
> *"What is your sister doing that makes you want to call her a name?"*
>
> *"If she wore your shirt without asking, perhaps you can say to her, 'Sarah, when you borrow my shirt, please ask me first."*

Are you struck by how powerful short direct sentences can be? Read these sentences. Imagine using them in a discussion with your child. Can you see what's happening with this kind of dialogue, where you turn the situation from a potential screaming match to something else entirely? Where will these sentences lead your family? Directly to respect, honor and love. This approach allows you to think, reflect and choose, rather than just to react impulsively and emotionally. You are using your mission and values in a consistent way that gives each child a feeling of security within the family. The playing field is the same for everyone. It means we've all agreed on what we value. And that should begin to color the way we act with one another and in the world outside the family.

Exploratory Questions

You can practice exploratory questions with your children any time to get to know what they think, feel, need, expect and want. Ultimately the answer will reveal something about a value.

Let's see how this works:

Your child comes to you asking for something, anything; it can be a piece of candy, a new pair of running shoes or a trip to the bowling alley. The conversation evolves like this:

Child:	*"Dad, can we go bowling today?"*
Dad:	*"That sounds fun. What do you like about bowling?"*
Child:	*"It's fun, just like you said."*
Dad:	*"Sure, but do you like being with your dad, playing the game, listening to the music, eating the food...?"*
Child:	*"Bowling is cool with you, Dad."*

There you see it. It's *you*. You are what your child values. Having fun with you, playing with you, laughing with you, succeeding with you. It's all about the relationship.

So far, we've talked together about Mission and Values. It's time we talked about the third foundational element: Rules.

꧁꧂

YOUR RULES

I hope you are starting to see how Your Extraordinary Family is taking shape. Let me ask you another question: Now that you have explored your core values and what's important to your family, how are you going to help your children live those values? It will be through the clear setting-forth of your family's rules. Rules are the way we show respect for one another, in our words and actions. Rules give *security* (a very important word) to everyone involved. But the rules need to be well understood by your children and appropriate to their age and skill levels.

Defining Your Rules

A young child's world is usually quite rule-bound outside of the home environment. They learn as three-year-olds that there are rules in the sandbox. At four, five and up, they encounter rules in the classroom. These experiences beyond the home make the children ripe for learning consistency, expectations and rules within the family culture. They will be ready to hear, "That behavior is not how we do it. That isn't living by our family rules. Let's do X instead." What is most interesting, miraculous, adorable and inspiring is that first you begin with rules, and then when your children understand the structure, they apply their intelligence and even get creative. See what my girls recently said to me:

How I Do It
(and try to keep a straight face)

I have two daughters, ages 8 and 10. They've been raised with our family Mission, Values and Rules. Recently, I was in my car with the girls. They wanted to stop and get a snack on the way to school. Our eldest, Olivia, said she wanted cheese curls, and I encouraged her to get some yogurt or a protein-filled burrito, good mother that I am. My younger daughter said, "Mom, in our home we lift each other up, right?" And I said, "We sure do... how is that related to cheese curls?" "Well," she said, "since we are unique and special, if Olivia wants cheese curls, that is her wish – so you can lift her up by saying, yes." I smiled outside and laughed inside. Alexis sure had the concept down and her application of the concept was hysterical. We bought yogurt.

A "Do This" Style of Rule Development

At the start of this chapter I paid a pretend visit to a typical home, maybe your home, and asked the children what some of the family rules were. And I heard a lot of *don'ts*. It's so much easier to say to your children, don't hit, don't get up from the table without permission, and do **not** leave the house without making your bed. You may consider these very necessary don'ts, of course. You're being authoritative and firm, and you're leaving no room for debate about some important family behaviors.

But far more than needing to be told what *not* to do, your children need to be told what to do – and more importantly, *how* to do it. You want to raise thinking children, problem-solving children. Using a style that encourages looking forward, planning for what to do next – that is what we're about to discuss.

You're not bad parents if you operate with more don'ts than do's, but I believe you are losing a golden opportunity to use your rules to help your children grow into their life skills. You're missing the chance to show your children how rules and structure lead to opportunity and growth, not shackles and immobilization. What I'm suggesting as you develop your family rules is a *do this* parenting style.

Talking to Your Children about the Family Rules

The cool thing about this exploration is that you can discuss your family rules in a natural way anywhere you are with your children. You are not required to sit down and have a formal discussion of your family rules. Sprinkle the discussion in your every day life and have fun with it.

You can enjoy the multi-sensory experience of brainstorming about your rules, writing them down, or even modeling them in a homemade book or a video (see the Activities section at the end of the chapter for hands-on ideas). Chat about your family rules with your children over dinner, in the park, or in the car (don't overdo it until it feels like a chore, just look for those moments when it can be relatively easily brought into the conversation). Ask them what kinds of rules would help you to be a happier family. Ask them what rules they break that get them in trouble and what rules they observe that make them feel good. Wonder aloud if you break any family rules. I know I do, and I appreciate it when the children say, "Hey Mom, that's not how we live." Then I can revise my words, actions or behavior. I can even apologize when needed. That's not showing weakness, it's showing that you respect the family's culture of rules and stand by them. It reinforces the power of your rules.

Remember that young children don't yet know the words and concepts to express their feelings when behavioral expectations seem arbitrary or vague; instead, they act out or simply ignore the rules – and you both become exasperated. Maybe you've noticed this already. If you have, you're ahead of the game.

Need a little nudge to get the process going?

If you have trouble generating ideas, here's a very basic rule you might start with: "We treat each other with kindness and respect." In another form you might write: "We use our words and bodies respectfully."

Now, if your child hits or talks back, you can say "Hey, we live with respect. How could you do that differently to show respect?" Whether you parent a child who is four, six or eight, this is as simple as it gets.

What is now clear is that when you establish your Mission, Values and Rules, your family knows what they're all about. Your children are able to define for themselves, for their teachers and their friends, what kind of family they live in and why. And they can trust you, their parents, to live by the same rules. You're all on the same playing field, right?

Change You, Change Your Child

Your family's rules are meant to be for *everyone*, so be prepared for your little ones to be alert to your own words and actions. When you too play by the rules, it will pay big, positive dividends down the road, which you will see as you keep reading.

On occasion, I have encountered parents who want their children to behave well, but do not behave well themselves. These are difficult parents to intervene with, because they seem to believe that they can be rude and insensitive, and expect to raise children who are loving, rule-abiding, and compassionate. It just doesn't work like that. There's never a reason to tell a child, "You're a baby"..."You're a brat"..."You are acting like a girl," or even, "Go live with your dad, I've had enough of you." And it certainly won't help children to be kind and considerate themselves.

Making changes in our children means committing to change within ourselves.

* * *

One Family's Experience

Zeva and David have 3 children, ages 5, 7 and 11. Before I met Zeva she found herself yelling at the children to obey the family rules from sunup to sunset. She felt that her children knew the rules and were willfully disobeying them, yet they had never had a discussion of the kind of family they lived in and why. The rules, in large part, were decided on a daily basis by mom and dad, and David was leaving much of the "dirty work" to his wife. The children felt adrift in what seemed like an arbitrary world of *don'ts*. In this situation, even though there were rules, they were a bit of a mystery to the children.

After reviewing with me the strategies for developing a solid foundation, these parents realized that if they wanted their children to live according to the family rules, they were going to need to define the rules *with* their children and then live in accordance with them as well. These smart, caring parents learned that **there are no one-way streets in effective parenting.**

Since Zeva now ascribed to the idea of *Change You, Change Your Child*, she made three rules just for herself:

✦ I will use a calm voice.

✦ When I am frustrated I will take 3 breaths.

✦ I will sit down and enjoy my children as they play for 20 uninterrupted minutes a day.

She posted them on the fridge and on her bathroom mirror. She told her children that she had a personal goal of living in a happier family and that she was going to try to live by her personal rules for the entire week. She even asked her children to help her by modeling the rules for her so that she could have living examples of the positive behaviors. Smart mother!

Zeva found that by setting new rules for her own behavior, her home became calmer and she experienced more joy. She kept the rules up for three weeks and was surprised one day when she realized that she was actually exhibiting her desired behaviors most of the time without looking at the fridge. Excited by this technique, she changed her rules in the fourth week and started to learn a whole new set of desirable behaviors. She was no longer parenting with frustration or anger every time a child did something she didn't like.

SUMMARY

You and your children deserve to live a happy life. That life takes some thought and planning. It starts with taking a moment to enjoy one another, to affirm that you are all in this together, and that is a wonderful thing. It takes developing a family culture supported by a foundation made of your Mission, Values and Rules. It only takes about ten minutes to engage in a quality conversation with your children about the kind of family they wish to live in. Imagine if every family spent just ten minutes on a regular basis reviewing what kind of family they wished to be and how to be all that they can. But it's not just a matter of how much time you spend, it's what you do with those quality moments.

Before you know it, you will be designing your family life rather than being led by it.

As you've read this chapter, I imagine some thoughts and ideas have started percolating already, and that is a wonderful beginning. Regardless of your personal family style, you are now a family contemplating and discussing who you are and what matters to you.

The following activities are designed to help you and your family turn those free-form ideas into a firm foundation.

Note: If you prefer to go directly to Chapter 2, please do. These activities pages will be here waiting for you when you're ready to explore some hands-on family projects for creating your mission statement, values list and rules.

HANDS-ON WITH THE FAMILY COACH

Making Your Family's Foundation Something Tangible and Fun

Recently, after I had spent an evening with one family discussing their Mission, Values and Rules, I arrived back at their home the next week to see an amazing bulletin board hanging in the kitchen. Working together, they had posted family photos showing valued family experiences, and then written their family mission at the bottom in gold paint. Up either side of the board were pillars made up of the family's values and rules, written in beautiful turquoise calligraphy. And the children had added their own handwritten statements. This family had applied their ingenuity and creativity and they were so proud of their fine work – for good reason. They told me that after I had left them, the conversation had gone on for days, and I believed them.

Now your family might be visual too, and you may create a beautiful board, or fill your family room with pages reflecting your communications and conversations. But I don't expect everyone to rush out and buy gold and turquoise paint. You may be more of a list family, writing neatly on white notebook paper, or you may just be conversational and decide not to draw it out at all – though I think it's very useful to create something you can actually stand back and look at from time to time.

ACTIVITY #1

❧

Create Your Own Playbook

One of the things that has helped the families I work with the most is the actual creating of their own The Family Coach Playbook. Families tell me that when they take the time to print out the exercises, post up their Mission, Values and Rules and put them in the Playbook, it helps them to do two things:

+ Keep their family culture "front of mind."

+ Monitor their progress and success.

There are many exercises, activities and thoughtful tips in The Family Coach Method – and you'll see that I often encourage you to write them down or draw them. I encourage you to use these items to create your own Playbook and keep it on your kitchen counter for quick reference, and to document your family's development. It is great fun to see how much work you have done and how far you have come by opening up your Playbook and reflecting on your successes.

How I Do It
(Of course The Family Coach would have her own Playbook!)

My family's Playbook is a 3-ring binder we keep in our kitchen on the counter. Personally, I like to copy and print pages from this book and put them in plastic cover sheet holders, so that each section of the Playbook is distinct. I am going to show you now what we keep where in our Playbook. Of course, you organize it as you wish; it is yours.

We've divided ours into 4 sections:

Our Foundation. This section contains notes we have taken at family meetings, drawings, planning sheets and agreements. It contains our family mission, our family values and our family rules. As things change over time and the children grow, we grow the foundation to reflect the current realities of our family.

Skill Building. Here, we have our green light, yellow light and red light lists (you'll learn about these in later chapters), notes from our conversations on "How we do it" and copies of articles we have found in other books and online to keep our tools fresh and lively.

Our Family Relationships. We keep things relating to our activities as a family, including copies of movie and event tickets we have saved, journal notes on the fun we have had together and any contracts we have made about our behavior.

The Family Coach Toolbox. The Family Coach Method is filled with specific tools for living a better, happier life together. This section is where we keep the tools together for easy reference. It's our essential Toolbox. Sometimes each child gets to write their notes about the tools we are using as a family. As an example, we have a rule that we do not use swear words in our home. So our daughters got creative one day and wrote a list of words they could say when they were angry that did not violate our rule. That was really cute and I even use some of their words now…"You're being a porcupine. Can you soften your quills!"

We also have our Mission, Values and Rules hanging on our pantry door. Some families have made their Playbook into a journal, others have taken large marker boards and hung them in the playroom or family room. That was enough for them; they felt they did not also need a binder.

What is really great about The Family Coach Method is that you take what is meaningful to your family and make it your very own. So give it a try. Whether you make a binder, folder, marker board or simple 8½ x 11 pages to hang in your home, your Playbook is yours now and forever.

ACTIVITY #2

Create a Family Mission Statement

As I discussed in this chapter, your family mission is a statement about who you want to be, together. For some families, it's about where they want to go or what they want to accomplish; for others, it's a statement about what they believe in most of all. When you have created your mission statement, each of you should be able to finish the sentence, *"We are a family who..."*

Perhaps you've started talking to your partner or your kids about what kind of family you are. Maybe at the moment, you're putting some early thoughts into a journal. Whether you've got some idea of what your mission statement will look like, or just haven't got the foggiest idea, I'd like you to start a conversation now, with the understanding that you will have created your very own Family Mission Statement by the time you're done.

If you have a partner, I recommend beginning with him or her first, just the grown-ups for now. Or you may want to spend a few minutes by yourself, with pen and paper. Here are some questions to get the juices flowing. You may answer them or simply reflect on them and take note of what comes up:

+ Is our faith or spirituality important?

+ Are we committed to some cause?

+ Do we have a strong belief in a particular code of conduct?

+ What are the guiding principles we/I want the children to grow up with?

+ What do we want others to think of when our family name comes up?

+ What are the things we want our family to accomplish?

+ Looking back in 10, 20 and 30 years, how will we know we created the kind of family we are proud of?

Are any of your responses starting to look like a mission statement? Does anything jump out at you as a particularly meaningful aspect of your family life or aspirations? Your answers will reflect your particular family culture.

After you've spent a few minutes (though you can take all the time you like!) pondering these questions, see if you can come up with a sentence or two that sums up your family culture, based on the ideas you've just generated.

Can you put this in the form of a mission statement? Write it down. Go ahead and write a few versions if you like, and see how they feel.

Bring in the kids

Invite the children to the dining table or the den or any place that feels comfortable to all of you. Go ahead and throw some pillows on the floor, perhaps. I recommend putting out some crayons or colorful markers along with some big sheets of newsprint paper for jotting your ideas down.

Go through the same list of questions with your children. Since you've just answered these questions yourself, use your discoveries to help them find and formulate their own responses. This is a great opportunity to explore what words like, *Faith, Principles* and *Hope* really mean.

Do some of their answers surprise you? Take note of those things that you didn't expect. And give yourself a little pat on the back when your kids show wisdom beyond their years. Share your responses with them and see if they agree. Remember, there are no wrong answers.

I encourage you to let your kids disagree with you. Take the time to find out why they think the way they do and let them know why you think the way *you* do.

Now that you've had a chance to hear what they think, bring out the draft mission statements you wrote earlier and consider whether they still sound good to you. If so, show the kids and get their feedback. Create a few more draft mission statements, based on your conversation so far, and toss them in the pot.

The Long and Short of It

By now, you should have had a fun and lively conversation. You and your kids should be feeling pretty enthusiastic about who you are as a family, and have some pretty good ideas for a mission statement. Look at the drafts you've got and try to winnow them down to a few finalists. Consider combining two or three and ask if that feels good to everyone. When you've found a few sentences that just fit, well then, chances are you've got your Family Mission Statement!

For practical purposes, you may wish to create a short version and a long version. The short version is the one you and your children can recall easily when daily decisions are made. The long version should include examples of particular behaviors that help your children fully understand your family mission. For example, if your family mission is, "We are a family who brings out the best in one another," additional statements might look like this:

"We will encourage honesty and fairness."

"We will support one another during hard times."

"We will praise one another's efforts."

Write it down

Put your mission statement to work by writing it down and putting it up somewhere prominent, like on the 'fridge or the family bulletin board. Children will feel especially invested if they get to create the document and decorate it themselves. And I wouldn't mind at all if you too picked up a crayon and added some artistic touches.

Draw it

Speaking of crayons, etc... I personally like using the symbolic image of a house to reinforce the purpose of the family mission (and values and rules). You can ask your kids to draw a simple picture of a house, leaving space along the bottom to write your mission, and space at either side to fill in with your values and rules. Your picture can be a vivid, visual reminder that your Family Mission Statement is the all-important floor that supports your values and rules, and everything you do as a family. You might end up decorating the walls with every-one's favorite activities.

Review it

However you document your Family Mission Statement, be sure to review it regularly to ensure that you're living up to your mission together.

ACTIVITY #3

꒜

Identify Your Values

Creating your Family Mission Statement is great practice for the next activities. In the same way you did before, I'd like you to take a few moments to reflect and then jot down the words that come to mind when you think about your values. As I mentioned, these are typically nouns – but not necessarily. It will always be up to you to decide what constitutes an authentic picture of your family at its very best. Your values may include things like *kindness* or *honesty*, or they may be more obscure, reflecting your particular family culture. The values that work for your family may not work for your neighbor's family – perhaps they place great value on *neatness*, while you value *creativity*, even if it means decorating the walls with finger painting.

If there are things you disagree about, or things that matter to you and not to your partner, take time to talk about it. After all, these are the things that make our relationships interesting! Are there ways that you can reframe your differences and find some commonality? For example, one of you may value watching the sun rise, and the other may value hard work, well into the night. Perhaps the point of commonality here is that you value making the most of your time together, while appreciating each other's interests.

Bring in the kids

Again, time for the colorful markers, crayons and paper, and inviting the children to a session of fun brainstorming and drawing. Initially, children may not feel they can identify their values as values, but it may surprise you that children as young as 24 months can tell you what matters to them and what matters to you. Begin by talking with your children.

Share with them what you mean when you talk of values, and give them some examples of things you value: for example, your love for them, your home, music, laughing. Ask them what kinds of thing they value. Do they value their friends? Their dog? Their grandparents? How about some feelings or experiences that they value? Fairness? Playing at the park? Love?

Here are some other questions to help guide your conversation with your child, age 3 to 8 (for your youngest children, you may need to adjust the wording). Pictures are a great way to involve your little ones. You can cut out pictures from magazines that represent what matters most to them.

- ✦ What kind of person do you want to be?
- ✦ What kinds of things do you notice about other people?
- ✦ Does getting good grades matter to you?
- ✦ Does helping others matter to you?
- ✦ Do you like to be a leader or are you more comfortable following along?
- ✦ Does making a mark in the world matter to you?
- ✦ Are there charities or causes that matter to you?
- ✦ Does being a good athlete matter to you?
- ✦ How do our actions reflect our values?
- ✦ Are there times when the things we do don't match our values? When? Why?

Expand the conversation and show you both understand and care about your child's perspective. Help guide your children with positive affirmations: *"So, having a say is important to you"* or *"Doing what you enjoy is important to you."*

Now transform your children's views into value statements. *"I am learning from you that..."*

"You value honesty."

"You value having a parent who supports you for who you are."

"You value showing your friends that you care."

"You value when Mom helps you structure your homework time."

"You value when Dad gets you to your football game on time."

This is another great opportunity to discuss the meaning of certain words and ideas. You can go over your list of values and tell your children why certain things mean so much to you. Or you can ask them what certain words mean to them: "family," "respect," "sharing," and so on.

Listen carefully to them and they will teach you a lot about what you are teaching them.

Learning to Listen

If you're up for an experiment . . .

For a few hours or so, I'd like you to activate your listening ears. Many of us are so busy instructing and directing our children to do this and that all day long that we forget to stop and pay attention to who they really are, how they think and how they feel – we lose the lovely *art of listening.* So now just try to stop talking and start listening. You'll be amazed at how such a simple act can change your relationships. If what your kids say surprises you, congratulations! You've got independent, thoughtful children. Go ahead, make the shift and see what happens.

Write it down

Get out those markers again and start writing down the values that you want to share *as a family.* Ask your kids what values they want to live by and encourage one another to live by.

Over the years, families with whom I work have come up with all sorts of values for their lists. I include only a partial list here as a cheat sheet of sorts.

Accountability	Flexibility	Perseverance
Attentiveness	Freedom	Professionalism
Balance	Forgiveness	Punctuality
Belonging	Followthrough	Reliability
Caring	Generosity	Respect
Closeness	Honesty	Reasonableness
Compatibility	Helping	Relationships
Commitment	Imagination	Responsibility
Communication	Initiative	Righteousness
Compassion	Integrity	Sensitivity
Confidence	Individuality	Spirituality
Cooperation	Joyfulness	Strength
Courtesy	Learning	Success
Courage	Leadership	Tactfulness
Determination	Listening	Teamwork
Devotion	Loyalty	Thankfulness
Discipline	Love	Thoughtfulness
Diplomacy	Motivation	Tolerance
Education	Modesty	Trust
Enthusiasm	Optimism	Understanding
Excellence	Organization	Uniqueness
Fairness	Patience	
Family	Peace	

Your list might be short or it might be long. It might be in prose form, rather than just a simple list. However you write your values, they are yours to model for your family (don't forget that part!) and live by.

Draw it

Once again, I encourage you to color and decorate your list of values. However you want to document your values, I suggest that you write at the top: *"AS A FAMILY, WE VALUE..."* and then list your family's values. Put it up somewhere your family can refer to and be proud of. If you are working on your drawing of a house, fill in the first column with your values – it's a great visual reminder of the important things your family is built upon.

Review it

As you go about your day, use your list to give meaning and substance to the things you do. For example, if your child doesn't understand why she has to go to her brother's boring school play, you can say, "Remember, as a family, we value celebrating one another's accomplishments." And your list will provide a visual reminder of this as well.

ACTIVITY #4

Identify Your Family Rules

If you've gone through the previous two activities with your family, you've done an amazing thing. Identifying and committing to a Family Mission Statement takes good communication, trust and love. Nice work. Now we're going to put your family mission and your values into practice by establishing clear, understandable rules for your family. These aren't just rules for the kids – though that's important – they're rules for everyone.

Write it down

With the family all together, I'd like you to take out a big sheet of paper and, on the left side, write down as many of your current household rules as you can think of. Chances are, you've got a lot of *don't* rules. Work together to figure out how to turn those *don'ts* into *do's*, and write the new, positive rules on the right hand side of your sheet of paper.

Here's what a typical list might look like:

NEGATIVE	POSITIVE
Don't hit.	Use your body respectfully.
Don't lie.	Be honest.
Don't cheat.	Do your work with integrity.
Don't ignore me.	Listen to me.
Don't make me tell you more than once.	Do as I ask you the first time.

Now talk with your children about why you have these rules, and why you want them to exhibit each of these positive behaviors. Look at your mission statement and talk about how your family rules help you achieve your family's goals. Are there other positive rules that you or the children wish to add to the list? Discuss why they might be helpful to your family or further your family mission.

You can also point to your values list and talk about how your rules give strength to your values. You can even make this a fun game: Ask the kids to match an item on the rules list with an item on the values list (there can be more than one right answer!).

Draw it

By now, you should have a pretty long list of positive family rules. Go ahead and write them out, decorating and coloring in any way you like – and I'd be thrilled if you filled in the second pillar in your house drawing (have the kids complete the picture with windows, doors, trees and a roof ... or anything else that is special to your family home).

Your list might be long or short. It might look something like this:

Our Family Rules List

+ Really listen when others talk.
+ Accept apologies.
+ Be humble in your actions and words.
+ Ask for help when you need it.
+ Brush your teeth twice a day.
+ Celebrate each other's accomplishments.
+ Keep your room clean.
+ Count your blessings.
+ We do as we say.
+ We raise others up.
+ Ask when you want to borrow something.
+ Speak respectfully of others when they are not there.
+ Tell the truth.
+ Let others finish before you speak.
+ Include others when you are having fun.
+ Accept correction gracefully.
+ Speak with an appropriate voice in the house.
+ Do what you are asked to do the first time.
+ Eat real food before sweets.
+ Exercise for our health.
+ Help around the house.
+ Keep dinner and homework times just for us (meaning that these are no-phone times).
+ Keep family matters private.
+ Keep your body private.
+ Use other ways than violence to express yourself.
+ Respect each other's personal property.
+ Respect each other's privacy.
+ Use our bodies and words nicely.
+ Respect our elders.
+ We say "I'm sorry."
+ We say "Please," "Thank you," and "Excuse me."

+ We share.
+ Take care of the cat – it depends on us.
+ Take responsibility for the things you do.
+ Wipe your feet before entering the house.
+ Try to look on the bright side.

Start with 3 rules

So now it looks like it's raining rules! A lot of rules right off the bat can be overwhelming. It's hard to keep so many in mind, 24 hours a day. So, with the help of your children, choose 3 rules, write them down and put them in a prominent place, like the fridge or the bathroom mirror.

You'll start by focusing on these rules first, and you'll track your family's success in following the rules for a week. This doesn't mean that all the other rules will be forgotten – this is not an excuse to conveniently forget that we go to bed early on a school night! The idea is to teach the skills they need, little by little, and to thoughtfully follow – and understand – the rules.

Review it

After a week, talk to your kids about how they think they did with these rules. Let them know how you feel they did, and how you feel you did. Then choose 3 new rules to work on. If you need to repeat a rule, that's fine, as long as your children understand why. Soon your family will have consciously practiced new skills for every rule on your list.

The purpose of this discussion is to teach your children that that they will become strong, thoughtful and happy people if they learn now how to live with positive behaviors, not negative ones. And let them know that you will try to do the same.

Note: From time to time, you may need to establish new rules to reflect your family's growing needs, or you will identify new values that are important. Like your mission statement, your rules and values will evolve with you.

CHAPTER 2

THE RULE OF RESPECT
(IT'S GOLDEN!)

༃

Now that you've delved into the concept of foundation, you're beginning to take charge of designing Your Extraordinary Family. No small accomplishment, even if you're still in the thinking-about-it stage. Take it from The Family Coach, you're already doing a great job – just for being willing to discover more about "who you are" as a family.

In the last chapter we talked a lot about family rules. I'm not quite done with them yet, because there is one rule that deserves its own chapter. It is in a category by itself and has its roots in the great religious traditions and philosophies of the world: the Rule of Respect. You may know it better as the Golden Rule, but its essence is the same...doing unto others as you would have them do unto you. Actually, this isn't only a religious concept, it's a societal one. It is what makes for harmonious transactions on every level of life, from building trust in the ways of the marketplace to preventing wars – everything. So you can see why I'd want us to pay particular attention to the Rule of Respect.

Respect is a learned behavior

Respect is a fundamental aspect of loving, trusting relationships. But since we are not born with an instinctual understanding of respect, we must learn it. That's where you come in. Through modeling this essential virtue in words and behavior you teach your children exactly what respect is and how they can feel, experience and show it to others.

When it comes to imparting the meaning and importance of respect, you are your children's first line of knowledge, learning and awareness.

Sometimes the word *respect* conjures up images of being strict or even dour. It doesn't have to be. I see respect in a much more positive way. When we interact with one another in a respectful manner we open opportunities to develop kind, trusting, caring relationships. Respect opens the door to love and trust in relationships.

What does respect mean to you?

Respect can mean a lot of things. Certain cultures view respect in a very formal, hierarchical way; others view respect as something earned, offered and more flowing. Respect looks different in the military or the police than it does among teammates or in a social setting. Respect can mean a feeling, placing another person higher on the social hierarchy, behaving in an obedient manner, doing what others in authority tell you to do, or interacting politely by using manners. What is important is how your family defines respect. How we show respect within our own family naturally determines how we show respect to our elders, teachers and friends – and to everyone else we encounter in our lives.

It is useful to reflect on what you mean when you say respect. Consider the following questions:

✦ What does the word trigger in your mind? (the first thing that pops in)

✦ Think back to a situation where you showed respect – why did you choose to be respectful? Did your respect for authority, the kindness a person showed you, or your belief that people will treat you as you treat them, affect how you showed respect?

✦ Think back to a situation where you did *not* show respect. What evoked this feeling of disrespect in you? What made you not respect that person?

✦ How do you view authority figures? Is it easy for you to respect authority or do you like to challenge it a bit? Why do you think this is?

✦ When you tell your children to "respect someone," what do you really mean by that?

As you ponder these questions, you might be formulating your own definition of respect, based on your own experiences and beliefs. Whatever you decide, it's important to understand what you really mean when you talk to your family about respect. Here are some ideas that have resonated for families I have coached – and with my own family – over the years. Maybe they do for you too:

Respect Is...

Respect is an attitude. It is an experience of honor, esteem, consideration, and caring.

Respect can be for oneself, for another person, for another being, and even for a valued inanimate object, such as a piece of art or a hand-made musical instrument.

Respect is paying thoughtful consideration to another person's words, feelings, thoughts, ideas, wishes or needs.

Respect is a feeling as well as a behavior.

Respect is revering or honoring another person. When you respect someone, you not only appreciate them for their standing in society, you might place them in a position above you on a feeling level or in practice. As an example, if you respect your grandfather, you may allow him to be seated at the dinner table before you sit down as a sign of respect.

How I Do It
(dotting the "i's" before a sleepover)

In our home, we often have several children spend the night on the weekends. Before the girls have friends over we discuss what respect means in our home. I remind them: Respect means letting your friends choose what activities they wish to participate in at our home. It means sharing your toys and not bossing your friends around. Respect also means that when I have cleaned the house, made the beds and prepared dinner for everyone, you do your part – we clean up our spaces as we play, we make the beds up in the morning and we sit politely for dinner without saying, "Mom, I don't like what you made for dinner." We show gratitude for one another so our home is a pleasant place for our friends to visit.

Taking that small amount of time to be proactive about the Rule of Respect has smoothed the way for many a successful sleepover!

What to Tell Your 3-year-old vs. What to Tell Your 8-year-old

Your vocabulary and your expectations will be expressed differently for each of your children. The concept of "respect" needs to be portioned out according to their individual developmental skills.

> ✔ **Example:** For a 3-year-old, respect might mean keeping your hands to yourself when you are in line at pre-school. For an 8-year-old, respect might mean remaining seated and raising your hand before you speak in class.

That seems easy enough. But sometimes, when stresses build and children are not behaving well, parents can lose sight of a child's developmental ability to comply with an expectation. The parent can become frustrated and the child is left confused. Just try to stay alert to what's possible for your child.

For Your Toolbox: *The Do-Over*

A do-over is one of the most effective tools a parent can use. It gives the child the opportunity to use new words or behaviors to get a better outcome. It isn't punishment, it doesn't lead to confrontation. It lets your child know that there's a better way to negotiate an outcome.

Don't like the behavior you've just observed? Stop and say (for example), "That behavior isn't working for me. Let's have a do-over. Show me what you want (or what's wrong) in a more respectful way."

Animals and Others on the Social Hierarchy

The most natural thing for you as a parent to do is teach your children to respect their elders, teachers and others above them on the social hierarchy. It's equally important to teach them respect for younger children, family pets or other animals (like the bunnies that may be scampering freely in your neighborhood). You want your children to show respect on many different levels. Even though your children are still young, they do have power over other more vulnerable beings, and so it is important to instill this sense of awareness as early as possible.

Reinforcing the Meaning of Respect

When you teach your children what respect looks like in words and actions, you're helping them master a vital life skill. It's time now to create a few sentences that you will actually say to your children in order to reinforce what respect means in your home. Tell your children clearly what it means to live with respect. Here's a sampler to get you started:

"Respecting one another means we use kind words and calm behaviors."

"Respecting our friends means listening thoughtfully to their wishes."

"Respect means that when a schoolmate criticizes the clothing another child wears, you tell them that we all have different taste and that we should be kind to our friends by choosing not to speak if we have nothing kind to say."

* * *

Question: **What is the best way you can teach your children to respect themselves as well as others?**

The Family Coach Answer: **By being a model of that "golden" behavior yourself.**

Model respect

Now that you have taken the time to think about what respect means to you and how your family members show respect, you are in a good position to be mindful about how your everyday actions line up with your beliefs.

If you wish your children to be respectful, let them see you be respectful to others as you go about your days. Respect must be a fundamental aspect of your family culture – *make it an expected behavior*. I can tell you with certainty that children feel secure with directives, but (and this is important) your child *must* understand that these directives are part of who you all are as a family. If you are confident enough to assert that, you will live with respect in your home and beyond, your children will do as you expect, and they will be proud of it. Most importantly, they will learn how important it is to carry this value into the world.

In order to create this outcome in your interactions with your children, you will need to model respect by your own actions and words:

✦ If you tell your children it is respectful to use a gentle tone when talking to one another, do you also monitor your own tone?

✦ If you tell your children to say "please" and "thank you" to the people with whom they interact, do they see you doing the same?

Be clear what you mean when you ask them to show respect. Do you want them to show respect to their dad? You can't just tell them, "Be respectful to your dad," And expect them to understand what you want of them. Your children learn what that means by watching *you* interact with Dad. You can even demonstrate what respect for Dad would sound like – this is a great type of modeling. For example, let them hear the sentence, "Dad, can we play ball outside now?"... instead of "*Daaad*, I told you to get the ball!" Guide your children, educate your children and model for your children.

Show your children respect (walk your talk)

One of the best ways to teach your children respect is to show them respect. *Showing* respect is different from *modeling* respect. Showing your children respect means using polite, kind and caring words and actions in your everyday interactions with them. They will learn from this both that it feels good to be respected and that you, the parent, walk your talk.

Honestly, showing your children respect takes some self-awareness. You might need to contain your tone, words and comments. You might need to curb your tendency to feel frustrated, angry or tired. Even when you're maxed out with life's daily demands, it's still so important to learn how to respond calmly, slowly and politely and develop those interactive skills that your own parents may have been unable to share with you. It can be hard at first, but it's so worth it! When you show your children respect you will raise more confident, masterful and cooperative kids. Respectful kids rule.

Maria Bailey is co-founder of *Momtv.com*, a valuable resource for everyone's parenting toolbox. Maria Bailey is also the author of *The Ultimate Mom*, and she has a tip for us about teaching respect.

How I Deal with Interruptions
(the secret handshake)

Children seem to love to interrupt moms, particularly when they are speaking to another grownup. Here is my surefire way to limit the interruptions, or at least manage them a bit more: Create a secret handshake with your child. It might be two short squeezes of the hand, or one long, one short. Make it fun. Tell your child that this is your secret sign that you use to tell the other person you need to speak to them. You promise that even if you are talking to an adult, you will find an appropriate part of the conversation to let them know that your child needs to speak with you.

Then, next time you are in a conversation with an adult, your child comes up to you and rather than interrupt, the child can take your hand while you are speaking, give it the secret squeeze, and you can excuse yourself from the conversation to address his or her needs. ("Excuse me, but my son/daughter needs to tell me something.") The secret squeeze is cool to your child and allows you to demonstrate proper etiquette to your child. **M.B.**

Trust is the foundation of respect. Showing respect for your children helps them develop a sense of trust in you and with others. When you trust a parent or a teacher to be polite with you, listen to your needs and take your thoughts and actions seriously, you learn that trust and respect go hand-in-hand.

Within the first few years of life, your children will have many opportunities to experience the feelings and behaviors of respect. When your children experience being respected, they in turn learn how to feel and show respect. As with any important life skill, this one starts at home.

Seven Signs of Respect

Consider when and how you live the following signs of respect in your relationships with your children:

Be a good listener. Give your children your undivided attention when they are speaking to you.

Be fair. Consider your child's viewpoint and experience before stating your opinion.

Be honest. Tell the truth. Be accountable when you make a mistake.

Be polite. Use the manners that you expect of your children.

Be positive. Focus on the positive side of life. Your children deserve a role model who "lifts them up." Compliment your children; observe what they do well and celebrate it.

Be reliable. Keep your promises. Show your child that you mean what you say and act on what you say. Children see the truth through a clearer lens than adults.

Be trustworthy. Keep your children's personal feelings and experiences private. Show them that you can be trusted to care about their feelings and their self-esteem.

Be alert for "teachable moments." As you move through your daily life in everyday situations with your children, notice when others are respectful, and comment about it. Identify how the child who waited his turn on the swings was living by the rule of respect. Point out for your children that the man calmly waiting for the waitress to serve his breakfast without rushing her is showing respect. This shows them how much such a behavior is valued and appreciated.

A Teachable Moment About Self-Respect

Has it occurred to you that when your children complete their homework and turn it in on time, that is a sign of respect for their teacher? But more than that, it is also a sign of a child's own emerging skill of self-respect. Let them know that you can see how they are respecting themselves by these actions. Tell them what a good thing that is.

When you teach your children to respect themselves, they in turn will learn to appropriately respect authority. A person who does not have self-respect can fear another, he can even obey another, but he cannot respect another.

Raining On Your Children

Some of you might have grown up with a "do-as-I-say-not-as-I-do" style of parenting. If so, you may have felt that you couldn't fully trust the people in charge of your life. When you have grown up with distrust in your primary relationships, sometimes it is difficult to learn a new way of interacting. You may experience moments when your pain rises up, and you react to your children in a manner you later regret. You don't want to act out on your children – I know you don't.

This can become a cycle of shame for you and your child if you do not learn to identify what leads up to these thoughts, feelings and impulses. I call this "raining on your kids." Raining on your children is using hurtful words or behaviors in your interactions with them. One of your roles as a parent is to "catch" yourself when you're not living with trust and respect – take a breather, re-group and come back with new words and behaviors.

If you experienced disrespect, mocking or lack of trust in your formative relationships, you might be in a process of expanding and developing your own style of communicating caring, trust and respect with your children. Perhaps even with your mate. Just by bringing your thoughts about trust and respect "front of mind" you are on the path to shifting your family and personal relationships in the direction of self-respect and respect for others. I applaud you for that. (You didn't think The Family Coach Method was only about your children, did you? This is just one more example of *Change You, Change Your Child*.)

❧

SUMMARY

I believe that respect is an attitude, feeling or experience that is learned – it is not innate. You are your children's first and most important teacher of respect. Be clear with your children about what respect means and how you expect your family to act respectfully in your home and in your daily lives. Talk about respect, model respect, and most importantly, live respectfully. This is one of the most valuable gifts you will share with your children. Respectful children are successful children and respectful families are happy families. If yours is a family that truly lives by the rule of respect, then you are equipped to weather every storm, together, even if you don't get all the little details just right. The rule of respect is the key to good parenting.

*Important Note...a family 911: On occasion I have met parents who feel justified using sarcasm and mocking in their relationships with their children. Sometimes these parents were mistreated as children by their own parents, so they believe emotional cruelty is normal. They usually don't even define what they say or do as wrong – they may have become somewhat numb to it. Other times, these parents are simply ignorant or mean, but **never** justified. No matter what the origin of your beliefs, it is not acceptable to be sarcastic, caustic or mocking toward your children. Your children deserve respect. I view a repeated pattern of sarcasm,* *contempt and mocking in a parent-child relationship as emotional abuse. Words can hurt just as much as a fist can. If you or your children experience emotional cruelty in your home, get help from a trusted source or your pediatrician. No matter what's going on at home, there is no shame in seeking help.*

HANDS-ON WITH THE FAMILY COACH

ACTIVITY #1

Role-Play to Teach Respect

Role-playing can be amazingly fun and very educational, for your children and for you. It's so effective because it makes abstract concepts concrete. Through role-playing with your children – even 5 minutes at a time – you can practice living by the rule of respect. (Role-playing doesn't sound like "you"? Just give it a try. Trust me, your kids will get a big kick out of it. You might even look a little cooler in their eyes, but more likely you'll get giggles just for taking a chance with them.)

It's simple: just imagine any situation where you want your kids to show respect – but instead of lecturing them, you're going to make a game of it. They don't need to know what's really behind it, but it's OK to tell them, if you think they'll join in anyway. What are some of the everyday situations you'd like to help them anticipate through role-playing? You might make-believe practice having dinner at a friend's place, or negotiating who gets to go first on the jungle gym, or even just getting to know a new, nervous puppy – basically, any circumstance in which being respectful will make things a little nicer.

Now, assign roles to yourself and your children. For example, you might want to help your 5- or 6-year-old understand how to engage her teacher respectfully.

You start: *"I'll be your teacher. Who do you want to be? Anyone at all..."*

Kara: *"I'll be Jason, he's always getting in trouble!"*

You: *"OK, so now you're Jason. Jason, can you help me clear the craft table for a few minutes before you go out for recess?"*

Kara, doing her best impersonation of the infamous Jason, let's out an angry *"No!"*

You (stifling a giggle) say, *"Jason, that wasn't very respectful. How do you think that feels to me, your teacher?"*

Kara *("Jason")* thinks about it and says, *"Not very good."*

You: *"No it doesn't. And why do you think that is?"*

Kara: *"'Cause you asked nice and it's good to help your teacher."*

You: *"You're right! So, how about a do-over! I'll ask again: Jason, can you help me clean the craft table before you go out to play?"*

Kara: *"Yes, Ms. Jefferson. I'll help you."*

You: *"Thank you, Jason. I appreciate it."*

See how this works? It's easy to get your kids excited about this kind of learning because it engages their creativity, humor and their natural skills for playacting.

For your older children, you can get a little more complex. Let them write down different social situations on pieces of paper and place them in a shoebox. Shake it up and then have them choose scenarios at random for acting exploration.

ACTIVITY #2

✿

Charades
(more practice for real life)

In a variation on role-playing, you might ask them to act out what different kinds of respect look like – kind of like charades. You can even throw a few puzzlers into the mix for "bonus points."

Some charade starters:

"Show me an example of how you will exhibit respectful words and behaviors to your teacher."

"How about showing your sister how you welcome your friends."

"Let Dad hear what you say to your karate teacher to be respectful."

"You are at the playground and a boy pushes a girl out of the way to get on the slide. How do you handle that respectfully?" (Definite bonus points for this one...)

"We are at a restaurant and a family behind us cuts in line. How do you respectfully tell them it is our turn first?"

This is practice for real life – for the rest of their lives, actually. There is nothing more difficult for your child than to know that you expect certain behaviors from them, but they don't yet have the words, skills and actions needed to exhibit those behaviors. The very best way you can equip your children is to **model**, **practice** and **play**. Through you, they will be learning about compassion, caring and, most of all, respect.

Ideally, this should be fun for *all* of you. Get into it and show your acting chops – or lack thereof. Let out your inner ham. And remember, being respectful is a skill we never stop learning. Both you and your children will learn a lot more about respect through these role-playing games and your interaction with one another than from any stern lecture.

ACTIVITY #3

Quiet Time
(thinking and writing about respect)

Do you have a child who likes to write his thoughts privately, rather than ham it up with his siblings? When the two of you are talking quietly together about the subject of respect, you might suggest that he write a short story about a time he showed respect, or a time when someone respected him and his wishes and needs. You might even open your own journal or notebook and write a story too, and each of you can read yours aloud. This can be a very effective way to practice being mindful about respect.

ACTIVITY #4

☙

R-E-S-P-E-C-T
(Aretha would be proud!)

Take some time over dinner or after homework is finished to talk as a family about what respect is to you. Think about your Mission, Values and Rules and ask your family what things you do or think that demonstrate respect. And – yes, it's time once again for the crayons and paper – write it and draw it!

You can just scribble your family definition of respect on a sheet of paper and put it on the 'fridge, if you like. But I recommend making this a family activity. Make an artistic cut-out of the letters R-E-S-P-E-C-T or write it out in big print with lots of color. Then, write sentences that describe how each letter stands for respect.

How about making an art project out of it by hanging the letters from ribbons in a doorway? Or make it 3-D: build a cardboard house and write on the walls sentences describing how each person shows respect in different rooms of the house ("Knock before entering Mom's office," "Ask to be excused from the breakfast table," etc.).

Here is how one family like yours defined respect:

Responsibility – We are responsible for our words and actions.

Expectations – We state clearly how we expect one another to behave.

Sharing – We value sharing as an essential part of our relationships.

Practice – When we make a poor choice we practice using new words and behaviors to make a better choice next time.

Everyone matters – We value each person's unique contributions to our happy home, and treat everyone we meet with kindness.

Cooperation – We cooperate to achieve our goal of living as a peaceful and loving family.

Togetherness – We value our time and relationships, so we make time for one another and we enjoy being a family together.

You will probably notice that there's a lot of overlap between your descriptions of respect and all the ideas you brainstormed in Chapter 1. This is just fine, as you will be giving your family another opportunity to learn how your Mission, Values and Rules aren't just static concepts that live on the 'fridge, but are integral parts of happy, successful living. You also demonstrate to them that you too are in the process of learning and that you, as a family, are supporting this process in one another.

Most importantly, you give your children a framework for understanding why you are correcting their disrespectful behavior. When your kids call each other names, grab toys, or take things without permission you can remind them, "We are a family who lives by the rule of respect." They will know what you mean by this (even the little ones). You can then provide them the opportunity to "make a new choice," a do-over, using better words or more respectful behaviors.

Remember, when we parent we do so with words and actions. So if you post your expectations, make respect-based activities part of your everyday living, and you live in accordance with your values, respect becomes foundational: it is expected and exhibited by all, including you.

CHAPTER 3

LIVE WITH RHYTHM, ROUTINES AND RITUALS

❧

Sometimes I buy books from authors with whom I resonate, like Bobbie Sandoz Merrill, author of *More Parachutes for Parents*, and Ross Green, author of *The Explosive Child*. I get really excited about their books, run out and buy them and devour as much as I can in a few hours in one night – eager to pick them up again when I have some quiet time. The words stay with me and I immediately apply the lessons learned in my own home. Really, I do. Sometimes I marvel that we authors, without ever meeting, share similar words and concepts in our work. That consensual reality makes the terrain of parenting a common one. Upon reflection, I think it all comes down to love and common sense.

Then, my children come in and want to play a game or jump on the trampoline. I breathe and tear myself away once more. The book-of-the-moment will get placed on my reading table and a week later I'll find it in the cushions of the couch, where I left it after another all-too-brief quiet time.

As parents we're so motivated by the possibility of change for the better. I wrote *The Family Coach Method* with that in mind – to help inspire you to make changes from the moment you read a paragraph, even if you pick up the book and set it down a dozen times. So, if you have gotten this far, congratulations, you've done better than I might have. But guess what, you've done so much already that your family is probably happier than you were the day you read the first page. If that is so, I am thrilled. I am excited for you and for your children. Keep up the good work, apply your mission, live your values and communicate your rules. That is a very solid path to happiness.

> ☛ **TIP:** It's important to remember that we are imper-
> fect. I embrace imperfection and feel that if we are
> trying to be mindful and thoughtful about our par-
> enting, that is good all by itself. There is no perfect
> parenting in this universe! So, don't beat yourself up
> if some of these changes take a while to work. And
> please don't waste your precious energy thinking
> you're not doing it "right."

That said, if you have the patience, discipline, motivation and time to move on, let's do, because now the "edible," actionable strategies begin, and they do not end until the final word of Chapter 10.

❦

Rhythm

The Family Coach Definition: **Rhythm**

(n.) Rhythm is a durational pattern, often to a beat. Biologically, our bodies live with rhythm every day such as the circadian rhythms to guide our daily wake and sleep cycles. When you live with rhythm you live with patterns within time. If you regularly wake at 7:00 am, dress, brush your teeth, pack your backpack, and get off to school, that is rhythm. Rhythm plays a role in every part of our world.

Early on in life, children really care about one thing, their security. If their initial needs are met – they're well fed, changed and unharmed – then they're generally satisfied. But eventually they must begin to develop mastery. Mastery is the ability to meet *task demands* because one is equipped with the necessary tools. This is a shift – from being taken care of completely to gradually being able to take care of oneself. The key to taking care of oneself is the understanding that there are reliable patterns in life, and having a clear idea about what comes next.

This is why it is important to establish rhythm, routines and rituals in your family life, so that your children know "what comes next" and can begin to develop skills that will allow them to manage the constantly shifting expectations of everyday life.

You may be a flexible, free-form person without a daily rhythm or you may be a highly-structured person who approaches each day with a well-defined method to your madness. Both styles and everything in between is just fine! The way you are is great, I am sure of it.

What I am proposing is that if you are open to establishing and developing a regular rhythm in your daily life, you will bring more order and meaning to what you do as a family, and everyone will have a clear understanding of what is expected.

It is likely that your children will relish rhythm. Children between 3 and 8 years of age thrive on their burgeoning mastery; they are developing their competency skills and love to experience "I can do it" and "I did it" moments. Rhythm gives them something to gauge their success against: Yesterday it was a struggle, today it was a triumph, tomorrow she will take on her next challenge.

Children rely on rhythm in order to know what to expect next. Isn't your 2- or 3- or 4-year-old always wondering, "What's next, Mom?" and "What will happen if I do this?" If I put a plug in a socket, if I pull a phone off the counter, if I take this fork and throw it on the ground...what's going to happen? It's important to establish rhythm, so that your children not only understand what happens next, but are comfortable with sequences and change. Teaching your children that there is a rhythm by which their daily lives run helps them to establish categories of activities and experience order. In this way, their brains are able to prepare for transitions, and they learn planning, preparation and assignment of specific skills needed for each new activity, be it waking in the morning, getting dressed, or going to school.

"OK," you say, "now how do I concretely apply rhythm to my children's days?"

I propose a family schedule as a first step to establishing rhythm in your daily living. The family schedule is a central component or core feature of The Family Coach Method because it instills rhythm in your family.

Creating Your Family Schedule

Do you have a family schedule? Don't worry if you don't...we'll create one together. And don't be nervous at the very idea of actually *scheduling* your rambunctious family. My purpose right now is to help you observe the patterns of your life and see where we can make them more clear for your little ones. (If it helps the grown-ups too, that's just extra credit!)

Do you know what happens in your family Sunday, Monday, Tuesday, Wednesday, Thursday, Friday and Saturday? You may be pleasantly surprised to realize that some things happen at regular intervals. Your family schedule is the visual template of where you are and where you go each day: Mondays we go to school, after school we play soccer, then we come home for dinner and dive into our evening activities; Tuesdays after school we go to the park; Wednesday we stay home; Friday we play ball in the driveway after dinner.

Your family schedule establishes your daily rhythm. One big advantage to having a family schedule that everyone can look at is that you won't have to keep reminding everyone what they need to prepare for. It will be right in front of them, all the time. It is a simple, powerful tool for your children to develop self-responsibility.

I'm going to walk you through defining your family schedule. Let's begin with Monday. What time do you wake up? What is the first thing that happens in your home? Perhaps you get up early to do some housecleaning chores before you go off to work. Maybe you get up early to check your emails before the kids wake up. You might sleep in because you work the nightshift. Now look at the rest of the week. What do you do consistently, either daily or just once a week?

Here are some activities that may (or may not) make up your weekly schedule:

- Chess
- Cleaning
- Cooking
- Dinner
- Family playtime
- Gardening
- Grocery shopping
- Meal planning
- Services
- Soccer practice
- TV and hobbies
- Work
- Writing

Starting to Make it Visual for You

There are lots of ways to represent your family's schedule. Here's one I like. It's simple and there's no right or wrong about it:

For Your Toolbox: *Assembling the Pieces of Your Family Schedule*

If you wish, you can start by taking out some markers and paper and then drawing lots of ovals or squares all over. Then fill them in with some of the activities that make up your week. You might even prefer a time-line. Sometimes I make shape diagrams (like the old bubble charts you used to write fourth grade papers) on the top of a posterboard with a time-line below. What matters is that now you're creating a picture of your days right there in front of you. Laying it all out like this can help you feel more organized because you can see it. When I can draw out the parts of my week I begin to see a pattern to it – a rhythm. I feel like now I can move the pieces around and actually manage them better. Maybe I'll cut the shapes out and paste them on a poster board signifying what happens on what day and time. You might even take one of your ovals and throw it away, thinking, "I don't need that to be part of my week." Play with it, think it, ponder it. This is your life every day; what do you want it to look like?

When you have a schedule, you and your children know what to expect from day to day. This allows them to develop internal controls to manage themselves throughout the week. Knowing what comes next also helps children who experience challenges with transitions; it tells them what to expect. Now, if you wish to jump to the activities section at the end of the chapter, you can continue to work on your family schedule – or you can keep reading about rhythm, routines and rituals, and check back into the activities later.

Yes, but... *"There are times when it's just impossible to hold onto my family's rhythm. Not even close!"*

When We're Out-of-Rhythm

In the real world where we all live, there will be times when we are off schedule and it impacts our family rhythm. Some weeks we need to add a BBQ at school, visits with grandparents and an overload of homework to our schedule. Changes in our schedules are often because of fun or new activities, which inevitably lead to fatigue. By Thursday we are a little grumpy and tired. What do we do? Why, we rest on Friday. After school we grab a movie, order a pizza and spend the evening cozied up on the couch laughing and eating until we are stuffed. I find that re-grouping and relaxing is an important path to regaining our rhythm and getting back on track. Not everything needs to be regimented.

Rhythm and Its Underlying Elements: Routines

For the purposes of this book, your rhythm is the rate or pace at which you do things on a weekly basis. It's the big picture, the overall structure. Now, within the larger rhythmic patterns are many small events that also happen on a daily basis: These are your *routines*. If we were talking about music, rhythm would be the distinctive pace of a song that makes you tap your foot from beginning to end. Using that music image some more, routines might be the repeating groups of notes that make up the verses and the choruses. All those little but important activities that make up your day, your week or your year are your routines. I love routines and rely on them a lot in my own parenting.

❦

Routines

The Family Coach Definition: **Routines**

(n.) Routines are a sequence of activities or tasks that are done one after the other.

The Importance of Routines

The rhythm of everyday life is layered with routines. Routines show exactly what each activity within the day's rhythm will look like. Like notes in a song, they get you in the groove of your family rhythm, like: First we do this, then we do that, the next thing that comes...*da dum da dum*.

Most families who come to my office and say their lives feel really out of control tell me they have routines in their minds, but they don't have routines set in their everyday lives.

"Before I had children, I had many routines"

One mom with whom I recently spoke told me that before she had children her life was comfortably ordered with routines. She had routines for walking her dog, routines for what nights she ate Chinese food and routines for what TV shows she watched at night to unwind. *"But now that we have three kids, I feel out of control, like my entire day is just chaos."* I think some of us can really relate.

If you want to put a little more order back into your days, consider the value of routine. The first step is to start with simple routines. If we begin in the morning, what's the first thing that happens? The second? The third?

What makes up your day?
+ Time to wake up, get dressed and go to school
+ School time
+ After-school activity time
+ Daily chores such as doing the dishes and making meals
+ Weekly chores such as grocery shopping and raking the yard
+ Homework time
+ Dinnertime
+ Outdoor Play/Sports time
+ Bath time
+ Reading time
+ Bedtime

If you are taking a step toward organization and order in your home, first consider your routines. Next, help your children with their everyday routines. Make them simple and discrete.

Early Morning Routines

You might wish to define a separate routine for each child or keep them all the same, depending on your style and family needs. If you have one bathroom, for example, you might stagger getting up, getting dressed and morning bath routines so that your hallway is not the site for an early morning family feud.

I notice that children understand things in groups of 3's and 5's, so you might begin your early morning routine with the first three things that happen in the morning: you get up, make your bed and eat breakfast – 1-2-3. It's very simple. After the first three are established you can add three more: You get up, make your bed, eat your breakfast...and get dressed, brush your teeth and grab your backpack...and you're done. They will begin to experience mastery and competence by knowing what they need to do and accomplishing their daily tasks.

> ☞ **TIP:** **It may help your children if you get them each a marker board and write out the morning and evening routines for each child. Then hang the boards on each child's bedroom door. They can check their routines each morning and evening to see exactly what comes next.**

Your children need to know what is expected each day and in what order

In the morning we:

✦ Get up

✦ Make our beds

✦ Get dressed

✦ Eat breakfast

✦ Brush our teeth and hair

✦ Gather up our school things

✦ Leave for school

In the evening we:

✦ Do our homework

✦ Eat dinner

✦ Clean up

✦ Play sports outside

✦ Bathe

✦ Read

✦ Go to bed

Each daily event has some routine as well. Each time you sit down to breakfast or dinner, there is some routine within the dinner experience (setting the table, passing the potatoes, asking to be excused). Things happen in a certain order. If this seems like a pipe dream, read on. I can't count the number of parents I've worked with who just shake their heads in disbelief at the idea of, say, having a nice, orderly dinner hour with their children. Then they cheer when we look back and reflect on how quickly dinner became a huge success!

Let's observe rhythm and routines in practice, through the experience of one of the families I worked with. Maybe parts of this story will sound uncomfortably familiar, and other parts will give you hope.

One Family's Experience
Establishing a Dinner Routine

I recently met with a family who felt that their everyday life was unmanageable. After establishing their Family Mission, Values and Rules, we went to work on establishing their routines. Dinnertime felt the most chaotic, so we started there.

Though the children were now in elementary school, the parents had never been able to get them to sit down for dinner. Dinner was crazy. The children complained about what the mother cooked, they got up from the table several times, and they ran off to their rooms afterwards without being excused.

These parents had to get back in charge of dinner. First, they needed to indicate when dinner begins and ends. Then they needed to identify who has to help with after-dinner cleanup and who can go outside to play, or to their rooms to finish their homework.

1. We clarified the expected routine. We wrote out the dinner routine and hung it in the kitchen.

   ✦ *Set the table.*
   ✦ *Place the food on the table.*
   ✦ *Sit down to dinner.*
   ✦ *Ring the dinner bell to mark the start of the meal.*
   ✦ *Say an observance of gratitude.*
   ✦ *Eat.*
   ✦ *Talk about our day.*
   ✦ *Ring the bell to signal the end of the meal.*

2. We marked each child's eating space at the table by taping off the space with wide blue painter's tape. We had each child draw on a plastic placemat to help them feel

ownership of their space. And we told them that once they sat down they would not leave that space without parental consent.

We placed hula-hoops under the children's chairs to further mark their "eating space." They were told that once the family sat down to eat, they were not to leave their eating spaces until they had asked permission and it had been granted by their parents. *Note: all of this "telling" is done in a calm, pleasant, direct tone that conveys to the children our expectation that they will comply.*

3. We told the children that they would need to ask for consent to leave the table.

To the surprise of the parents, when dinner was done, the children asked for permission to leave the table. Once they were excused, they took their plates to the sink, and went into the living room for family activities. Wow. Dinner became peaceful and orderly. The parents just looked at me, dumbfounded. For the next hour, we played together and did a family drawing. Then it was time for a bath, reading and bed.

Now, for the first time, this was a family who understood what a dinner routine looks like. There were clear expectations and a clear beginning and ending. Afterwards, they were able to spend time together as a family.

Your children depend on routine. They need to know their routines and they need to know what's next, because this helps them with mastery. They also hunger for you. Not just your 3-year-old or your 8-year-old, but even recalcitrant 'tweens will do activities with a parent if the activities make sense and appeal to them.

Insuring Buy-In: Collaborating to Create Routines

When you take the time to talk with your children about their daily routines you secure their interest and commitment to their daily tasks. When a child can tell you what they need to do after they brush their teeth or take their dishes to the sink, they experience pride in knowing what's next. Collaboration – including your kids in the talking, thinking and planning – lets them feel a part of your plan. In the business world this is called *buy-in*, but it just means your children feel heard and included, and thus more likely to comply. As adults, we're no different. Would you rather be lectured at or invited to problem solve? What would make *you* more eager to participate? That's buy-in.

Rituals lend warmth, creativity and memories to your family life. Let's look at how rituals can enrich your family life.

Rituals

The Family Coach Definition: **Rituals**

(n.) Rituals are a repeated pattern of activities that you do the same way over time.

Children lean on and are comforted by their rituals. Rituals also slowly lead to the development of habits. Help your children develop healthy habits by having consistent and intentional rituals. A ritual is a consistent pattern of behavior exhibited during a specified time-frame, life experience or season. Rituals can come on a daily basis, they can come on a weekly basis, they can come on a monthly basis, or they can come at specific times during the year. Rituals can be anything from laying out your clothes the night before school, to what you say or do on a religious holiday.

How My Mom Did It
(and I never forgot)

A long time ago, my mom created a ritual for our family. When we took down the Christmas tree, we would have hot chocolate and ginger bread. I'm telling you that even when I was twenty-five, the night we took down the Christmas tree I wanted that hot chocolate and ginger bread. I still do. It makes me feel warm inside and connected to my family. That's enough for me to know how important it is to give my own children the gift of family rituals.

So think for a little bit. Where do rituals fall into your life? Is it a Friday night Seder? Is it Sunday morning brunch? Is it playing music every Monday night? Is it a special evening once a week where the children get to choose what food you eat? Each Earth Day do you share a green gift to represent your dedication to green living? It can be anything that has meaning to you as a family. Think about this and ask often: "What would be a very simple ritual we could do?"

One practical ritual would be sitting down to a hearty breakfast – that's a really great way to start your day. What about waffles on Sundays? Rituals don't have to be grand ceremonies at all.

How about reading to your children at night while they bathe? Tell stories, practice math or talk about what they've done during the day.

When your third grader is more interested in the computer than you, instead of creating a situation where you are fighting about this every day, create a family ritual that takes care of the problem naturally and positively.

You can create a Saturday afternoon hiking ritual, and take the whole family to a park or the creek (maybe with a stop for ice cream on the way home). Afterwards, your child can be free to get on the computer for an hour. They might balk at first, but once this has become a ritual, you'll all be in sync.

Rituals: The Family Security Blanket
(getting through hard times together)

There are times when families go through extra-stressful challenges: losing a job, serious illness and death, to name a few. As parents we may think we're pretty good at keeping our worries from our kids, but children actually feel our tensions far more than we can sometimes see. It is especially important during those times to try to maintain as much of your family's rhythm, routines and rituals as you can. This will have a calming effect on everyone, parents and kids alike...think of it as your family's familiar, reassuring security blanket.

SUMMARY

Chances are, before today you already did observe certain rhythms, routines and rituals in your life, but just hadn't thought of them that way. They are important tools for teaching your children how to manage change. Starting with a family schedule gives your children a comfortable, predictable place in which to start developing skills, and the routines and rituals further develop order and mastery. Always remember that your children will carry the skills you model in your family with them, long after they have left the nest. Even though it's a long time in the future, be aware that what you do now is giving them the template for one day creating their own Extraordinary Family.

HANDS-ON WITH THE FAMILY COACH

ACTIVITY #1

Develop Your Family Schedule

As adults we're used to just *knowing* what happens when, and how long it should take, that we don't even think about writing it down. We know that we need to get up at 6:30 to give us enough time to bathe, dress and eat before we catch the 8:15 train to work. But young kids don't have all this stuff hard wired yet. That's where a nice, clear and concise family schedule comes in. A family schedule that you can refer to, together, every day will help build this skill in your child.

Just the act of writing down your family schedule – what it currently is or what you'd like it to be – will tell you a lot about where there might be stress or problem areas, or successful moments, as your family goes through its day. You'll be able to see where there's room for improvement or where expectations may or may not be clear. As we've already seen, getting clear about your expectations is a key component to creating competent kids.

> ☛ **TIP:** Head to your local teachers' store and get color-coordinated poster boards for your schedule, routines and task lists. These "decorator" versions will be pleasing to the eye.

To create your own family schedule try this:

Use your posterboard, graph paper or a plain white sheet of paper to begin developing your family schedule. Write the hours of the day down the left side and the days of the week across the top. You'll be filling in the grid with your family's activities. Just start at the beginning. How long does everyone need to bath and dress? Do you like to go for a run? Write it down. How much time do you need to give to breakfast? What time do the kids need to walk out the door to catch the school bus? And so on .... You might leave some times intentionally open, like lazy mornings on the weekends or Friday nights. That's fine too.

What does your family schedule look like? Does it look like a good balance of time, energy and structure? Or does it look impossible for a mere mortal to follow? Or is it almost empty?

Beyond just considering how workable it is, look at it and ask how you are building and nurturing your relationships during the course of the week.

By now you should know that I'm a big fan of poster board and colorful markers. There's a reason for this: Getting kids involved in the actual creation of these family tools gives them a sense of involvement and pride in your work together – that buy-in I mentioned. It's also a lot more appealing for a child to refer to a colorful, wonderful piece of art than something drawn up by an accountant.

So, once you've got your preliminary schedule worked out on paper, put it into a form that your kids will be attracted to. Transfer your schedule to a large poster board or a laminated schedule from a school supply store. Get everyone involved with decorating it. Then hang it in a prominent place such as the kitchen wall or in the back hall to let your children see what their everyday lives look like. This schedule is a picture; it's a symbol; it's an outline of your life in print.

☞ *TIP:* **For your smallest children who don't yet read, you can use Velcro-backed cut-outs to represent the different activities throughout the day. Stick the pieces onto your schedule board and allow your children to take them off and place them in a special envelope when they've completed a task.**

It's always helpful to see how others have approached this. Here's a sample schedule that the Marino family created. Lacey is 8 and JC is 3:

OUR FAMILY SCHEDULE

TIME	MON	TUE	WED	THUR	FRI	SAT	SUN
6 am	Exercise		Exercise		Exercise		
7 am	Breakfast	Breakfast	Breakfast	Breakfast	Breakfast		
7:30 am	AM routine	AM routine	AM routine	AM routine	AM routine		
9 am	Lacey School	Lacey School Mom and JC Playgroup	Lacey School	Lacey School Mom and JC Playgroup	Lacey School	Breakfast	Breakfast
10 am						Lacey Soccer	
11 am							
Noon							
1 pm	JC Nap	JC Nap	JC Nap	JC Nap	JC Nap		
2 pm	Clean house	Make calls	Clean house	Make calls	Clean house		
3 pm	Pick up Lacey	Pick up Lacey	Pick up Lacey	Pick up Lacey	Pick up Lacey		
4 pm	Homework	Dance Class	Homework		Dance Class		
5 pm	Cook/Play	Cook/Play	Cook/Play	Cook/Play			
6 pm	Dinner	Dinner	Dinner	Dinner	Pizza Night	Date Night	
7 pm	Family Games	Family Games	Family Games	Family Games	Family Games		
8 pm	Bedtime Routine	Bedtime Routine	Bedtime Routine	Bedtime Routine	Bedtime Routine	Bedtime Routine	Bedtime Routine
9 pm							

For Your Toolbox:
a Family Communication Center

We have spoken a lot about creating your own The Family Coach Playbook, where you can keep your notes, observation, tools and activity sheets. I just wished to mention that I have worked with a few families who created a Family Communication Center in their kitchens. You might buy a marker board with a cork section so that you can write a schedule, hang notes regarding routines and keep family rhythms and rituals "front of mind." Beneath the Center you can have a collection of stationery and office supplies labeled for ready use. You can even communicate with your partner and kids about special upcoming events and schedule changes in your Family Communication Center.

ACTIVITY #2

※

Develop Your Family Routine

Your schedule (Activity #1 above) should contain some very general items, letting you each know where you are on the day's timeline. Now it's time to break those items down to their component routines. For example, "bathe and dress" consists of a number of discrete tasks and skills: "clean face and brush teeth," "put pajamas away," "get dressed" and "brush hair."

To create your own family routine list, try this:

Consider making a routine list for each child that you can post on their door. Erasable noteboards or felt press-ons will allow you and your child to check off the items on the list each day to give your child a sense of "I did it!" accomplishment. Again, your children will enjoy being included in this process, and they will be very happy to take the fruit of their labor – in this case, a personalized, decorated routine list – back to their rooms to refer to each day.

* * *

Here's an example of the Marino family's routine list:

OUR FAMILY ROUTINE

ORDER OF TASKS	Name LACEY	Name JC	Name
Morning	Rise at 7 am	Rise at 6 am	
Task 1	Get dressed	Cartoons	
Task 2	Eat breakfast	Eat breakfast	
Task 3	Brush teeth/hair	Get dressed	
Task 4	Pack backpack	Teeth/hair	
Task 5	To school	With Mommy	
Evening			
Task 1	Clean up after dinner	Play after dinner	
Task 2	Do homework	Bathe	
Task 3	Bathe	Read	
Task 4	Read	Bedtime	
Task 5	Bedtime		

ACTIVITY #3

❦

Create a Ritual: "Family Date Night"

There is nothing more fun than going on a date with your children. OK, maybe going on a date with your partner is fun too! But when you have date night with your kids you get to know them individually in the context of a close one-to-one relationship. How about if you create a family ritual where one Friday night per month you go out with one of your children and your partner takes care of the rest of the kids or babysits the dog back home. You can switch off. (No partner handy? A babysitter, friend or grandma will do nicely. You can even suggest swapping date night duties with another parent in your neighborhood!)

Another idea: When the whole family goes to the mall – or to a movie or bowling – pair up one of your kids with one adult, and another with the other adult...and start your date from there. If you have four to five kids, divvy them up between you. This new constellation will bring out opportunities for lots of fun and laughter.

Have each child create a list of activities he would like to do with you. Keep it in your binder or journal, or better yet, in your The Family Coach Playbook. In just a few hours each month you will build a lifetime of memories together.

How I Do It
(and love every minute)

When a new movie came to the theatre one week, we invited a friend and her mom to sit with our older daughter and I sat with our younger daughter. We all watched the same movie then met for lunch afterward. What a blast!

II

TEACH YOUR CHILREN SKILLS WITHIN THE CONTEXT OF YOUR RELATIONSHIP

Allie

CHAPTER 4

CREATING ACCOUNTABLE, MASTERFUL CHILDREN

❧

The transition from toddler to child is a leap for both of you. As a parent during this time, you go from meeting all your toddler's needs to helping your 3- to 8-year-old learn to be independent and responsible for herself. This is one of those profound developmental processes that no one really teaches parents how to navigate. But that's why we're here now, to help you and your child develop the skills you'll both need to enter this amazing and challenging time in your lives.

Small Steps to Wider Horizons

When we speak of responsibility and independence, we're really talking about mastery and accountability. In other words, your child is free to wander a little farther away from you at the park because he has mastered the skills required to do that: he stays within bounds, he engages with other children respectfully, and he knows basic concepts of safety. And he has shown you that you can rely on him to do these things as you expect – this is the accountability part. The level of independence you give him, and the accountability you expect in return, will grow as your child grows. Children as young as 3 are beginning to feel their own way in the world, with your guidance.

But how do you introduce independence and responsibility to your children? First, you provide your child with the opportunity to exhibit a greater level of skill than he has previously. You might make the conscious choice to stop picking up your son's underwear from the bathroom floor and expect him by age 3 or 3½ to put them in the laundry basket himself (He'll feel like such a big boy!). You start to break down specific tasks and activities of daily living and allow your child to do more for himself. These are often small tasks for an adult, but brand new and perhaps even exciting to a child.

As you clean your home or fold the laundry, begin identifying small tasks that you can give your child so that he can feel more sense of accomplishment and mastery. Don't worry too much if he gets it wrong at first – he will master his new skill quickly.

The Family Coach Definition: **Task Demand**

(n.) A task demand is a set of expectations that require a certain level of skill to complete. The task demand is what is required of you to complete an action. The skill is what is needed to meet the requirement. Examples of task demands would be: 1) being required to wait to walk out the door when you are really excited and your parent tells you, "Wait until I say you may go outside." 2) being required to put your hands in your pockets before you get near a brand new baby. 3) needing to hold a pencil correctly in order to write your name. 4) needing to shift one's attention from the television to the parent, when the parent says, "Turn off the TV."

If you haven't already noticed, your 3-year-old is capable of several chores around the house. She can pull up the covers on her bed, pick up toys and put them in the toy bins, take her laundry to the laundry room, pour water for the family dog, wipe up his messes with a paper towel and even help you dust. Watch the transformation from toddler to skillful 3-year-old as your child proudly helps you and herself.

✔ *Example:* **When your 3-year-old asks for milk, you say, "Let's look on your shelf in the 'fridge. Do you see it there?" Voilá! Before your child, right at eye level, is his cup of milk, pre-made (of course you were ready for the request!). "You can take it and drink it." In this simple scenario, your child now experiences pride at being able to do this on his own for the first time.**

By the time a child is 5, he is ready to hear, "You are really growing up. You want to do many things like play at the park, ride your bike on your own, and stay up later. You may be ready to do those things, but with independence comes responsibility." These are big concepts for a child, but ones which they are primed for and often quite ready to understand. It happens with small steps.

Your 8-year-old has better dexterity, is taller and can think through tasks better than a 3-year-old. He can help you fold laundry and put it away in open drawers. He can set the table, clear the table and he may even love vacuuming. Your job is providing the opportunity to complete these tasks, but his experience will develop solid skills for a lifetime. As always, don't expect perfection and give credit for a thoughtful effort.

☛ *TIP:* **If you want to suggest improvement, frame it in the language of success: "You did a great job folding those shirts! Would you like to see a little trick for making it even easier?"**

Independence and responsibility go hand in hand

With the independence of sleeping in a "big girl" bed comes the responsibility of making the bed each morning. With the independence of taking the school bus comes the responsibility of placing homework, lunch and permission slips in the backpack, then leaving it in the "ready-to-go" position at the back door. With the independence of watching television one hour a day comes the responsibility of making sure homework is completed before the television is turned on. See how this goes?

When you tie independence to responsibility early in life, good habits that foster responsible independence become the norm.

Teaching your children this relationship early will lead to children who place their clothing in the hamper and not on the floor, teens who clean up their fast food when they return the car, and college students who always finish their studies before going out at night with their friends. As in adulthood, independence and freedom must co-exist with responsibility.

Demonstrate this now and your children will understand it forever. Responsibility may not be the message they're getting from the popular culture around them, but it's the message they're now getting from their family culture...and you're taking the proactive measures to establish your family culture strongly in your children's minds and hearts. Is it worth the effort? You bet it is!

The Importance of Choice

Choices are one of your child's first introductions to responsibility. While choices appear to be about freedom, they are also about decision making, taking responsibility and committing to action. Choices can decrease control struggles, foster mastery and give you the freedom and time to make a change in your parenting approach as needed. Offering your children choices regarding what skills and actions they will use and how also helps them to use their problem-solving and decision-making skills. It is important in a family to allow children to make choices; this is a central part of helping them become masterful.

Here's a helpful "How I Do It" from expert mom and nanny Michelle LaRowe, author of *Working Mom's 411* and the *Nanny to the Rescue!* parenting series.

How I Help My Child Make Good Decisions

Kids love feeling like they have a say in what's going on, and one way you can help children make good decisions is by presenting them with two choices you can live with. So, instead of asking your child, "Do you want to go potty?" tell them, "It's time to go potty," and ask them if they'd like to read the car book or the bug book while they sit. Praise your child when he makes a good choice. It will empower him and encourage him to think for himself. **M.L.**

But you do not have to offer choices in every instance; some moments require a *direct parenting* approach.

The Family Coach Definition: **Direct Parenting**

(n.) Direct parenting is a style of parenting in which the parent tells the child what to do and how to do it. The child is expected to comply immediately. Direct parenting is a *"First I tell you, then you do it"* style of interaction.

Children can have choices about what they wear to school, what they pack in their school lunches, who they have over for a play date, what sports they play, what instrument they play, etc. I like choices and I give children many choices when I work with them. Now you may be looking at choices a bit differently than before. They are not to be offered willy-nilly, because choices require cognitive commitment on your child's part: *commitment to taking action.*

Choices are about taking responsibility

As you probably know already, choices can be messy. It takes time to think about options for our kids, and it takes patience to allow a child to consider, decide and then act on the choices given. I often meet parents who are having difficulty setting up their home environments to encourage independent skill development. Usually these parents have greatly curtailed their child's power of choice. This is an understandable hurdle in that transition to independence I discussed earlier.

As busy parents, it's sometimes a whole lot easier for us to just do all the daily family tasks ourselves. We can do it quickly and efficiently and we've got an eye on all the other things we still have to get done. I know, sometimes it drives you crazy to see all those toys on the floor or clothes strewn around. But if you always clean up after them, your kids won't get to experience the feelings of accomplishment and responsibility that come with taking care of their things.

A good way to start changing the impulse to do everything yourself is to think not about the inevitably haphazard job your 5-year-old will do when asked to help pick up leaves in the yard – but about welcoming your child as a valued and contributing member to your family community, and not sweating the small stuff.

When One Parent Does Too Much

In some families (well...a lot of families) one parent takes responsibility for more than a fair share of the family to-dos and ends up feeling resentful or overwhelmed. Taking the time as a couple to write out and discuss family responsibilities is good for the marriage or partnership and a great way to begin passing on responsibilities to the children. I also know that many, many households are headed by a single parent who may not have the luxury of turning to a partner and saying, "Honey, let's make it more fair because I'm having a hard time here." Everyone needs to know when it's time to reach for help.

My friend Bradi Nathan, co-founder of *MyWorkButterfly.com*, and founder of *ForYouTwo.com*, has a personal story to share with you:

How I Wish I'd Done It
(and listened to a friend's advice)

The best piece of advice a friend ever gave me was advice never taken: "Stop being a martyr!" You see, I have a husband who works, A LOT. And so, the brunt of the family and household responsibilities falls on me – a role I took on willingly some nine years ago when I left my six-figure advertising executive income to become a stay-at-home mom. Because I made the commitment to my family and to myself, I felt guilty asking anyone to help at a time when I desperately needed it. My friend told me to stop being a martyr when she saw me suffering rather than celebrating. If...just if, I had gotten the help of a sitter, or I had asked my family to step in earlier, I would have been a much better mother to my children, wife to my husband and kinder to myself. If you are overwhelmed by motherhood like I was, especially if your kids are young, don't go it alone. Being a mom is by far the hardest job I have ever accepted. And the most rewarding. **B.N.**

Now, let's get back to those family chores – and helping your child climb another rung up the skill-building ladder. In her book, *Nanny To The Rescue*, one of my favorite parenting authors, Michelle LaRowe, says, "Never do for a child what he can do for himself." To me, this means that your children need opportunities to exhibit age-appropriate skills. You're not being mean, you're letting them experience what they are capable of so they can continue to grow. This calls for some smart, savvy strategies on your part. Coming right up!

Savvy Family Strategy: The Clean Sweep

This terrific tool will enhance your child's sense of independence and responsibility – and work wonders in your home at the same time: The Clean Sweep. This is a 5-minute before-we-go-to-bed clean-up activity. In a way, it will serve as an example for many other strategies you will employ as you begin to transfer responsibility, mastery and accountability to your children.

In this strategy, there is a beginning, a middle and an end.

Beginning: You introduce the strategy to your children.

Middle: You all participate in the actions.

End: You review what happens as a family when you are successful or unsuccessful in living up to your responsibilities in completing the Clean Sweep.

If you recall, in Chapter 3, Rhythm, Routines and Rituals, I suggested an activity for developing a chart of your family's routine tasks, which would include routines leading up to bedtime. For The Clean Sweep I would like you to create a separate list that contains all the tasks that can be done in an evening to make sure the kids' rooms are clean before bedtime. Include the little ones in making the list in order to get that ever-important buy-in. They may even have suggestions you hadn't thought about before.

Here is a typical list I came up with of what needs to be done at the end of the evening so that your home is organized before you go to sleep. Your mileage may vary.

+ Put away toys.
+ Throw away any trash.
+ Make sure there is no food left out for the bugs to nibble on.
+ Put every object (pencils, papers, jewelry boxes, small objects) in their homes for the night.
+ Make sure folded clothing is in its proper drawer.
+ Lay out your outfit for the next school day.
+ Smile, because you know where all your stuff lives and how to find it.

So now you should have your Clean Sweep Task List. In order to help your children learn good habits, develop personal accountability and feel a sense of accomplishment, hold a 5-minute Clean Sweep every night in your home. Have the children run through every room picking up what they have left out that day. End in their bedroom where they complete their Clean Sweep Task Lists.

No need to argue or have a conflict over this; just have them clean up really quickly and tell them that anything you find still out of place goes into the Saturday Box.

The Saturday Box
a tip from a wise grandma
(The Family Coach can't claim authorship of this great idea)

The Saturday Box is a container you keep in your front hall closet. Anything you have found out of place – soccer balls, Nintendo DS's, CD's, etc. – goes in this box and it cannot be retrieved or used until next Saturday. Any child who values their computer games or dance music will be quick to put it in its "home" lest they lose it until the weekend.

The Buy-in: Typically, in order to get children to buy into a strategy like this, you may choose to give them the night off on Fridays and Saturdays. Only children who are neat-nicks will want to clean up every single day. But if you assign tasks and responsibilities for week-nights only, the buy-in should be strong. Most children like their possessions and will not want to lose them. And especially importantly, they will get the satisfaction of a job well done on a regular, daily basis. Acknowledge their success.

Assigning Daily Tasks to Encourage Responsible Behaviors

It's important to distinguish between appropriate choices and things about which there are no choices. Being a contributing member to a clean household with respect for all its inhabitants is not one of your child's choices; it's his responsibility. Therefore, certain tasks might be rules, based firmly in your Family mission and values.

> ✔ ***Example:*** **If you are a family who supports one another, you may have a rule that everyone pitches in to clean up after dinner. You can say, "This is how our family lives and this is what we need to do." And be firm about it.**

The majority of families I work with are facing a lack of control in their homes. The children refuse to do as told and parents feel their home lives could be better managed because peace and calm at home is noticeably absent. Fundamentally, when I work with these families, the first order of business is establishing a firm foundation of Mission, Values and Rules. If children are not clearly told what kind of family culture they live in and what behaviors are expected, then they are confused. Noncompliance is often the most common result.

It's easy to see now how the rhythms, routines and rituals work together with consistent messages about your family culture to develop masterful and accountable kids. When children know what's coming next and what is expected of them, responsible behaviors are the result. They become habitual.

For Your Toolbox:
The Routine Task List

Remember the Routine Task List from the last chapter? It's one of my favorite tools in The Family Coach Method. Task lists are essential for healthy family living. They serve two functions: 1) to help the family regain order and, 2) to help the children develop independent skills for health and wellness. Children as young as age 2 know that their life experiences have some order. A 2-year-old knows that when she sits in her highchair food is about to be served. This is the beginning of their understanding that some predictability exists in their world. Often, the first time I meet with a family we review what kind of family they wish to raise and then we begin to establish routines that will help them create the home they desire to live in.

The Routine Task List makes those routines stick. It is such an important part of The Family Coach Method that if you haven't created one yet, and still wonder why you feel like you're living in the land of chaos, stop reading this chapter right now! Check out Chapter 3, find the Routine Task List chart and create your own list. I'll be right here when you come back.

By engaging in ongoing dialogue, be it in your home or simply with yourself as you turn the pages of this book, you are now looking at your parenting experience differently. You are developing the tools to raise kind, caring, ethical and skillful children. Way to go! But a nagging question might keep popping up for you:

Yes, but..."*What do we do when things are not working as planned?*"

When Transferring Responsibility is Just Not Working

Some parents tell me that teaching their children to be more responsible causes stress in their homes. The primary concern they raise is that the children don't do as they are told. What to do when your amazingly tough daughter resolutely says "No!" or wanders away yet again from the mess she just made at the dining table? When you consider the brief list of things that need to be done before a child heads off to school or goes to bed, it doesn't seem that hard. So what gets in the way? Here are a few possibilities...with strategies for each.

✦ **Procrastination:** Children frequently delay completion of the task. There are so many other things children would rather do than get dressed and go to school, like watch TV, play video games, text friends, play with toys and listen to music.

✦ **Cognitive inflexibility:** Some children are quite resistant to shifts in activity. They become cognitively rigid and have trouble transitioning from one activity to the next. This can result in a tendency to become emotionally overwhelmed and melt down.

✦ **Parental distraction:** If you are a working parent with multiple deadlines, you have a lot on your plate. Getting yourself ready for work and making sure the children are on task is quite a job. We're human, we get scattered and tired, and we're not always 100% focused on our kids.

✦ **Skill deficits:** There are times when the skills expected of the child are beyond his cognitive or developmental skills. This can interfere with the ability of the family to move through their morning routine efficiently.

Whatever the cause, the first step in solving a behavioral challenge is to keep track of what gets in the way of your child behaving in accordance with expectations.

✿

Tackling Procrastination

If your child is prone to procrastination, help him learn to set appropriate goals for completing tasks. Follow these 7 steps with your child:

1. Identify for your child the discrete task that needs to be accomplished.
2. Break larger projects into smaller parts or action steps.
3. Write out the steps to the task and prioritize them.
4. Create a time frame with a deadline.
5. Develop the habit of "Do it now!" (see p.81 for the definition of "direct parenting")
6. Eliminate distractions.
7. Reward success. Never forget this one!

Using this list, let's apply it to two common situations. In both cases, the task demand (having the skill necessary for the task) is the same: Overcoming procrastination.

BEHAVIOR I: *My child is slow to get dressed in the morning.*

Step #1: Identify the discrete task that needs to be accomplished.

Parent*: "Elijah, the first thing you need to do when you get up in the morning is get dressed."*

Step #2: Break larger projects into smaller parts or action steps.

Parent: *"I'd like you to choose your outfit the night before and lay it on top of your dresser. Pick out your jacket, pants, underwear, socks and shoes and place them on your dresser. In the morning, it will be easy to get up and put your clothes on before you leave your bedroom."*

Step #3: Write out the steps to the task and prioritize them for your child...1-2-3:

1: Lay out your clothes.

2: Put your clothes on.

3: Leave your bedroom.

Step #4: Create a time frame with a deadline.

Parent: *"Please have your clothes on before you come down to eat breakfast."*

Step #5: Develop the habit of "Do it now!"

Parent: *"As soon as you get up, what is the first thing you need to do?"*

Child: *"Put my clothes on."*

Step #6: Eliminate distractions.

Parent: *"Keep your eye on the prize...time to get dressed!"*

Make sure that in your home the TV is off and no other children are allowed in your child's room to play before he gets dressed. Stand firm on this!

Step #7: Reward success.

Parent: *"Elijah, give me 5 for a job well done!"*

*   *   *

BEHAVIOR 2: *My child forgets to put her homework into her backpack.*

Step #1: Identify the discrete task that needs to be accomplished.

Parent: *"Julie, you are to put your homework into your backpack before you go to sleep at night."*

Step #2: Break larger projects into smaller parts or action steps.

Parent: *"We will place your completed homework on the kitchen counter so that you can put it in your backpack before you go to bed."*

Step #3: Write out the steps to the task and prioritize them for your child.

1. Complete your homework.
2. Put it in the homework drawer.
3. Mom puts homework on counter.
4. Julie puts homework in backpack.
5. Julie puts backpack in the bin at the back door.

Your verbal expression of these steps might look like this:

"Julie, I want you to complete your homework and place it in the homework drawer at your study desk. After dinner, I will put your homework on the kitchen counter. Before you go to bed please place your homework in your backpack. You will then put your backpack in the bin at the back door so it is ready for you in the morning."

Step #4: Create a time frame with a deadline.

Parent: *"Your homework is to be in your backpack before you go to bed."*

Step #5: Develop the habit of "Do it now!"

Parent: *"Julie, remember your commitment to put your homework in your backpack before you go to bed? Stand up and take action now.*

Step #6: Eliminate distractions.

Parent: *"Sweetie, I know you like to listen to music before you go to sleep. You'll be so happy that your homework is in your backpack before you put your headphones on."*

Step #7: Reward success.

Parent: *"You can be proud...your homework's in your backpack. Enjoy your music. I adore you!*

Tackling Cognitive Inflexibility

Task Demands

Every day, your children are faced with tasks they need to accomplish. Earlier, we defined task demands. Daily tasks often require sustained attention, application of skill-sets and completion of goals. Everything, from drinking from a bottle to getting dressed in the morning to studying spelling, involves task demands: *that which is required to complete an action.*

We take these sorts of things for granted because they're "no-brainers" to us. That's because we learned them at an early age. There was once a time when it was all new to us. So let's take a closer look at some of the things that stand in the way of your child's success with tasks, and what you can do about it.

Every time a child performs a complex task in a new environment, they have to learn to adapt somehow. This means they must interpret and understand the new environment and what changes are required in their behavior. No small feat in neurological terms, and for some children this kind of flexibility is harder than for others. In situations where children should be flexible in order to deal with changes in the environment but are not, their rigidity or inability to adapt their behavior is called cognitive inflexibility.

Cognitive inflexibility is not willful non-compliance; it is a skill deficit.

A cognitively flexible child is one who can...

+ Easily shift attention off the original or familiar task and onto a new one.
+ Identify new task demands.
+ Focus attention on the new task demands.
+ Determine what new behaviors are needed for the task.
+ Manage the anxiety or fear that may be associated with "brain shift."
+ Apply the new skills to the new task.

This whole process is important in childhood because it is one foundation of adaptability and learning. The critical part in enhancing flexibility is engaging your child in the development of the strategies for achieving the task – creating a buy-in. Participation increases compliance and competency.

When children are young, they are confident meeting task demands when the tasks are routine, because they practice and learn how to be skillful at the task in familiar circumstances. It is comforting for a child to be able to complete a task without frustration. When children who are cognitively flexible encounter new task demands, they are able to re-evaluate the new situation and adjust their skills to the new task demands without excessive anxiety. Not so with a child who is cognitively inflexible; she will simply be stressed out in the face of new situations.

How can you help your child to experience cognitive flexibility when facing new tasks? The Family Coach Method has had good success with the following steps:

1. Prepare your child for the new task. Tell your child the *what, when, how* and *who* of the task. Get her used to the whole idea.

2. Engage your child in creating the strategies to achieve and manage the new task. Ask your child what she thinks will help her achieve the task. Develop steps for achievement with your child's ideas in mind.

3. Review the steps to achieve the new task.

4. Practice the new task with your child.

5. Revise your words and actions based on how your child responds.

In Chapter 8 I'll be discussing the way a child's brain is working at these ages. Basically, there are two parts that affect behavior, the instinctual, more primitive part I call the **Caveman**, and the higher functioning, more rational part I call the **Thinker**. In the two behavior situations below, we will be trying to engage the Thinker.

BEHAVIOR 1: *My child won't sit in his car seat.*

The task demand: Accepting Constraints

Step #1: Prepare your child for the new task ahead of time.

Parent: *"Trevor, when we ride in the car, you need to stay in your car seat."*

Child: *"No car seat!"*

Parent: *"You are only safe in your car seat. It is the law. How do you want to climb into your seat...from the front or from the back?"*

Step #2: Engage your child in creating the strategies to achieve and manage the new task.

Parent: *"Before we get in the car, you can choose a toy to hold."*

Child: *"No toy!"*

Parent: *"Let's make a treasure chest for the car. You can keep it next to your seat."*

Child: *"Toys?"*

Parent: *"Let's go to your room and choose toys for your treasure chest. When we go to the car, you can choose a toy and play with it. You will sit in your seat for safety and play toys. Then we can sing the car song."*

Step#3: Review the steps to achieve the new task.

Parent: *"First we get our toys, then we get in our seat, and then you play and play the time away."*

Step #4: Practice the new task with your child.

Parent: *"Trevor, let's take the treasure chest to the car and practice now. Show me how fast you can get in your car seat."*

Child: *"Run!"*

You can use a stopwatch or timer to make sitting a task your child enjoys. Children like "beating the clock." As you practice sitting behavior, talk with your child about the toy, book or art supply he has chosen to keep his brain engaged. Allow your child some age-appropriate responsibility by allowing him to buckle himself in. Engage him with strategies to use his thinking skills while you are practicing.

"Can you make a funny face?"

"Do you see something red?"

"What sound does a dog make?"

"What should Mommy do with her seat belt?"

"Show me."

Step #5: Revise your words and actions based on age and how your child responds.

You will want to revise your strategies as your child grows. What engaged your child at fifteen months may not interest your child at twenty-four months. As your child's cognitive skills develop you will be able to engage your child by naming him "Car Captain" and assigning him responsibilities. Creativity is always allowed, so feel free to follow your child's lead into a little silliness if it works to bring efficiency and mastery to the situation.

Parent: *"Now that you are a big boy, you can be Car Captain and tell Mommy which CD we should listen to and what games we can play while we drive your sister Sarah to school."*
Child: *"Raffi music."*
Parent: *"That's a great idea. When you stay in your seat we will listen to Raffi."*

* * *

Behavior 2: *My child won't stay in his bed.*

The task demand: to stay in bed at bedtime.

Step #1: Prepare your child for the new task.

Parent: *"Lisa, we are making a bedtime routine to help you stay in bed at night. What will our routine look like?"*

Step #2: Engage your child in creating the strategies to achieve and manage the new task.

Parent: *"First we brush our teeth, then we get our pajamas on, then you get in your bed, and then we read a book. What do you want to do next? How about if you sing your goodnight song? And after that it will be time to say goodnight. Mommy will kiss you and then it will be time to stay in your bed."*

Step #3: Review the steps to achieve the new task.

"Brush our teeth."

"Put on our pajamas."

"Get in bed."

"Read our book."

"Sing the goodnight song."

"Mommy kisses Lisa."

"Lisa stays in bed."

Step #4: Practice the new task with your child.

Parent: *"Let's play goodnight and see how you get into your bed. Mommy will hang a goodnight chart on your door. I will put a sticker on it when you go to bed, and in the middle of the night when you stay in bed, and in the morning when I come to get you. When you have six stickers we will go to the dog park and see the doggies."*

Step #5: Revise your words and actions based on how your child responds.

How it Plays Out

Assume Lisa does not stay in her bed the first night. She climbs out and you find her at your bedside. You take her back to bed and tell her she will get a sticker in the morning when she is in her bed. The next morning when you go get her, you place a sticker on her chart and tell her you are making her "Princess for the day" because she stayed in her bed. Make a crown with her that she can wear to school, to the park, or to an activity you have planned for the day. Try to avoid threats, coercion or tactics designed to force her to do as you wish. She will learn over time that you stay calm and she is to stay in her bed.

Tackling Parental Distraction

Morning is a busy time for families. Parents need to get dressed and ready for their own responsibilities, yet your children need your attention. What to do? Establish some routines that allow your children to share time with you as you are getting your tasks done. Children from two years and up like to be a part of your routines. They can help you make breakfast, set the table, straighten up the house and get their own things ready. Maybe it is faster if you do it yourself, but this can leave your children frustrated with their own tasks or with nothing to do but make mischief.

If you need to get on your computer, make calls or complete your own responsibilities, set yourself up at a table with artwork, or create an activity they wish to do so that you can complete your tasks, but still be near your children. Try to manage your schedule of tasks in a way that allows you to complete your responsibilities when they are at school, with a loved one or sleeping.

Be mindful of when you are ignoring your children or leaving them out when you are with them.

I know from experience that it's not always easy, but *managing your time* is a critical part of staying present and avoiding distractions. It will – I promise – pay off in both work efficiency and a warm and comfortable relationship with your child that will last for a very long time.

❧

SUMMARY

WOW! Now you are really doing it: parenting with purpose and mindfulness. If you have already started implementing The Family Coach Method, are you seeing a difference in your children? Do you see how when you break down tasks and teach your kids how to tackle one step at a time, it really works? You can see that it is through your mindfully tended relationship that your children learn how to be competent and caring. And you learn, as well. So much of The Method is about Change You, Change Your Child.

Ready to dig deeper? In the next chapter we're going to focus on taking yourself out of damage control with your children, and into skillful compliance. Sound too good to be true? Read on. I have so much more to tell you.

HANDS-ON WITH THE FAMILY COACH

ACTIVITY

"My Daily Points" Tool
(for self-monitoring behavior)

You may know children who hit or call names, only to blame the other children for their behavioral choices. Sometimes these children blame others in order to justify their own behavior. More often, however, they have not developed the self-awareness, planning, and impulse control to manage their behaviors effectively. This occurs particularly when they are ages 3 to 8. One step toward helping your children follow the rules is improving their ability to observe their own behaviors and the impact of their behaviors on others.

Research shows that children behave better when their view of their behavior coincides with the view others have of their behavior. As an example, 7-year-old Juliette is more likely to hold the door open for her peers at school when her peers view that behavior as one Juliette is anticipated to exhibit. If asked to rate her "door holding" behavior on a scale of 1 to 5 (1 being poor and 5 being excellent) she is also more likely to rate herself as her peers would see her behavior, if she knows they are also evaluating her.

You can use self and sibling ratings as a tool to help your children observe and manage their behaviors better at home. The Family Coach "My Daily Points" tool can help your children consciously monitor their behavior. All you will need is a blank sheet of paper, either poster size or notebook size (you might want to keep this one in your Family Coach Playbook). Here's how it could look:

Child's name: _____

    Time _____   Points _____

    Time _____   Points _____

    Time _____   Points _____

Begin with three rules for your family to follow for one week. Each day, focus on one of the rules. Make a sheet of paper with each person's name across the top. On the left hand side write down five different times (such as 7 am, 8 am, noon, 3 pm, and 5 pm) representing what time your children go to school, camp, soccer, etc. Try to choose five specific times when you are with your children so that the rating period is based on times when you are present to observe behaviors. Help your children monitor their adherence to one family rule each day by taking a moment and asking your children, "On a scale from 1 to 5, how well did you follow the family rule today?" On the scale, 1 is poorly, 2 is partially, 3 is OK, 4 is good, and 5 is great. Those will be that child's points.

Let's put this tool into practice:

"This week, we will be focusing on three family rules:

(1) Being an active listener,

(2) complimenting one another, and

(3) putting our belongings back in their homes (where they belong).

Today is Monday, so we are working on 'Being an active listener'."

Take the time to help your children see where they are earning points with an eye toward what behaviors they wish to improve.

CHAPTER 5

THE BIG FOUR:
PLAN, PREPARE, PRACTICE AND PREVENT

꿰

It's easy for an over-stretched parent to start treating parenting as damage control – dealing with the crisis of the moment, just staying afloat until the next problem arises. Just *dealing*. Being reactive instead of proactive. But too often that can reduce parenting to two things: discipline and punishment. And that's not where you want to be. Parenting is about having relationships with and teaching skills to your children.

In this chapter I'm going to show you how to become a proactive parent and say goodbye to "just dealing."

The Family Coach Method Definition: **The Proactive Parent**

(n.) One who anticipates a potentially difficult situation or behavior and guides it to unfold in a constructive manner, rather than waiting to respond to it after it happens.

We all want our children to learn and exhibit skills that will benefit them as well as benefit the whole family, but what is the most effective way we can engage them in this learning process? By planning for a range of eventualities, preparing for success, practicing skills and preventing negative outcomes. It's not as hard as you might think. It's really a matter of getting a few key concepts clearly in your mind, seeing that there's a logical sequence to them and then giving them a chance to work.

What you are doing as a parent is creating a scaffold structure that your children can climb with and grow with on their way to self-mastery. In The Family Coach Method each concept builds upon the last. You have already met a number of core concepts such as: a) establishing a firm foundation, b) understanding skill deficits and c) change you, change your child. *I consider these to be "edible" concepts, because they are easily understood and digested.*

Let me introduce you to another of my favorite "edibles": **previewing**. This is a neuropsychological term that describes the ability to review all possible choices before you take action. (My colleague Paul Beljan, Ph.D., inspired this thinking.) That is what this chapter is all about – previewing what is needed, planning for the event and taking action to successfully meet potential challenges.

Families can feel off-balance and constantly stressed by trying to keep the lid on the latest emotional storm in their midst. Every day in my practice I see how previewing skills can help families restore a sense of equilibrium.

Climbing Out of Damage Control

Many parents I meet for the first time hang their heads in shame when they tell me about the true state of their family. They feel guilty that their children have skill deficits. They feel ashamed that their children bear "diagnoses" or are on medication. They pre-judge themselves in the harshest way before we even say hello. This breaks my heart. It also compels me to love what I do. Because I can help.

I can let them know that they are wonderful, caring, intelligent parents. I can assure these families that they are normal, that I am not here to criticize them and that we will find success no matter what our starting point. I can remind them that we do not choose our genes. No one comes out of the womb asking for a learning challenge or anxiety. We are dealt our genes, and then our environment and our nutrition bring what we are born with to the surface. It is how we *respond* to our biology that determines whether we develop into happy, healthy and successful individuals.

This will be an important chapter. It takes the concept of previewing and applies it to the real-world situations you encounter every day. I think of it as my Four-Step Family Recovery Program. It consists of **Planning, Preparation, Practice** and **Prevention**...the Big Four. If you follow the four steps below, you will be laying the groundwork for peace and happiness in your family (quite a promise, I know...but I'm standing behind it). You will learn how to avoid living in damage control. And best of all, you will be helping your children develop their scaffolding skills, those skills that build upon each other and lead to mastery.

Meet the Big Four

PLANNING: The act of determining what you will do in an upcoming event or experience.

If you run a family business, help in the PTA, work for a large corporation or prepare delicious dinners for your family, you already know what planning is. If you're planning to cook an amazing dinner, you look up the recipes that you want to use and know what ingredients you need to get at the grocery store before even beginning to cook. The same thing is true in parenting. It starts with a plan.

PREPARATION: Living in a state of readiness for a pending event or experience.

Preparation is making sure the necessary steps have taken place in order for you to execute your plan. This sets the stage for a successful outcome. If your plan is to get out the door on a school morning in a timely manner, the preparation is to pack the backpacks the night before and place them at the back door, complete with a protein bar (for emergency snacking), a bottle of water, finished homework and any signed permission slips for that day.

PRACTICE: Learning through the experience of repeating words or actions again and again.

Many of us introduce skills to our children at the moment they need them. A better approach is introducing the skill *before* it is needed. This gives your child the chance to exhibit the skill in a low-stress setting and then be ready the moment they are called on to use it. They will be more able to "call-up" and use the skill when it is needed.

Practice may involve previewing a specific experience with your child, such as a tryout for a sports team, or how your child uses language and social skills in order to choose a friend to eat lunch with. A highly effective practice tool is *role-playing* with your child in anticipation of a particular event or situation. (For an example of role-playing, see page 112.) Practice is an element that we often miss when we are parenting. This is likely because we feel our plates are already full just with getting through the day; taking time out to deal with things that aren't right in front of us seems like a luxury. But it's practice that brings forth a higher level of skill development and skill execution, and it's practice that makes us better able to manage all those little "surprises" that can overwhelm us.

PREVENTION: The act of taking the steps to ensure an expected behavior is exhibited without negative consequences.

Prevention involves helping your child anticipate and meet a new situation or challenge. Let's consider an experience many of you know well, introducing your toddler to a new babysitter and trying to prevent the "falling apart" scene when you leave. If you typically introduce your child to new care providers you are probably already familiar with this concept and intuitively take some preventive actions: 1) You introduce your child to the sitter in the comfort of your home prior to leaving your child with the sitter, 2)

You clearly communicate your toddler's routine to the sitter so that the rhythms and routines of the day match what is familiar and expected to your child, and 3) You define a consistent ritual of transferring the care of your toddler to the sitter in a loving and safe manner.

Let's take them one at a time, in depth and step-by-step.

✿

Planning

Put planning into action

Many of us have specific behaviors in mind that we would like our children to exhibit: We want them to do their homework in a timely manner, we want them to do a task when we ask them, we want them to adhere to their bath schedule, we want them to clear their dishes after dinner, or (in the not-too-distant future) we want them to return the car full of gas.

We have lots of behavioral expectations of our children, but in order for them to successfully exhibit the skills we are requesting, we need to develop a plan that will help them succeed.

Start talking

Planning can start with a conversation about what is expected. This can happen at lunch, at dinner, in the car or anywhere else, but you must communicate the behavioral expectation in advance of the situation so that your child can become familiar with what you're expecting. That's the first thing you do. You've got a goal in mind and now you're going to plan the path to take – whether you want to help make an event run smoothly for your child, or to help your child accomplish tasks and daily chores.

> **☛ TIP:** So often we talk to our children from another room. **Good communication with your children means getting up close. Talk to your child face to face at his or her level. Teach your children how to look you in the eye when you are talking. Get close to them. You might touch their chin or shoulder to alert them and make sure you have eye contact when you are speaking.**

Take the mystery out of it

Planning is especially useful in helping your child anticipate and cope with new experiences. When your child experiences fear of new experiences – anxiety surrounding using a skill set or difficulty with specific skills such as planning, organizing and thinking tasks through – you can do any of several things to help: You can role-play with her, or sit down with her to write a story about what will take place, or draw pictures to help her plan what she'll say or do. You can make a recording of a story about it; little ones love this. You are taking the mystery out of the upcoming experience and making it familiar and safe...maybe even fun. Most of all, you are helping your child start to think ahead and develop the concept of planning. And never forget: Your child is learning from you, too, as you model your own skills.

For me, planning, preparation and practice are "sprinkling skills in your child's life," meaning that anywhere you are in a given day is an opportunity to teach your child about planning – to have a real, two-way conversation about what to expect and how to plan, prepare and practice for any upcoming experiences or events.

How I Do It

When I am teaching a child a skill set, I break the skill set into three easy steps. I then sprinkle the beginning, middle and end of the experience as we are actually doing it. So, as an example, when I am at a park teaching a child how to focus on one activity at a time (improve his sustained attention) I say, "Lorenzo, first we agreed to play on the slide, then we went down the slide, now we are going to do it again before we go play on the swings."

* * *

Many of us have children who participate in music, art or sporting events. Planning for any activity that will require coordinating both your child and your family members takes some thought.

Planning Scenario #1: *"Let's get ready for the soccer game."*

Let's consider planning for a sporting event. The first step to planning includes the conversation about the upcoming experience. "We're going to a soccer game as a family, we're going to meet your friends, and we're going to be there all day, so I'm sure we're going to be hungry. What's our plan about having lunch that day?" Your child might say, "I think we should bring sandwiches," or, "I like the hot dogs at the sports complex." Have a conversation about it: What's the plan?

Discuss how you are going to have lunch. Talking about the plan then helps you with some preparation. What if the water bottles at the sporting event are $2.50 apiece, but you can buy them for a dollar at the grocery store? Do you want to bring a cooler with water? Do you want to have a plan to bring sandwiches? Do you want to have a plan for one child to make the sandwiches and another child to pack the water bottles? Your children will enjoy developing a plan. It helps them to feel secure about an upcoming experience.

Planning Scenario #2: "Pick up your clothes when you take them off after school."

When your children come home from school and change from their school clothes into their play clothes, what do you want them to do with those school clothes? How are you going to communicate to them that you want them to pick the clothes up off the floor? You can't just expect them to do it (though sometimes you might get lucky). Remember, your role is to communicate clear expectations so that they can then do as you ask. So you might say, "When you get home from school, you will take off your school clothes and place them in the hamper. Then you will put on your play clothes."

So the planning part is making sure the hamper is accessible to your children. This might include placing hampers in their bedrooms so that they can easily place their clothing in the hamper when they change. Planning can also include a period of observation in order to see who's putting their clothes away and who's not.

Overall, planning includes the conversation, the thinking and the looking forward. The plan leads to knowing what you will actually need in order to execute the plan successfully. Now we've come to the second step: Preparation.

Planning Strategies from the Classroom

Working in schools with well-organized teachers has really informed both my clinical and parenting skills. Because teachers essentially "parent" 20-40 children at a time, they need to plan out lessons, label items, work off schedules and lists and prepare for many unforeseen events. If you have time, attend a teacher training on managing a classroom in your school district or at your local community college. You will be amazed by what you learn.

Preparation

Get into the Preparation Habit

Preparation is simple once you have a plan. Returning to the theme of going to a sporting event, consider what preparations you need in order to have a successful experience. You may want to:

+ Bring water for everybody.

+ Bring sun block.

+ Bring sun hats.

+ Bring chairs for everyone to sit on.

+ Bring the appropriate clothing and equipment for the event.

+ Bring snacks to eat.

+ Bring a change of clothes, if appropriate.

The preparing is actually having a checklist, packing the car for the sports event, making sure the children have their duffle bags with all their sporting equipment and checking off the list as you put everything in. This might be an opportunity to enlist your "assistants" to call out, "Check!" when an item is stowed. Remember, they're planners-in-training. Over time, they can take on more and more of the preparations with you (I'm betting they'll want to), and you won't always be the one standing there on the driveway with the checklist and 100% responsibility for what goes into the car.

Now that you've talked about your plan and prepared for an upcoming event, the next step is practicing for the upcoming event, previewing for your children what challenges they might encounter at the event. This can take place well ahead of time or just before, depending on the kind of event. Again, the idea is to create in your child a secure familiarity in advance of a new experience.

Practice

Put practice into play

Your role as a parent is to help your children practice, or rehearse, particular experiences they may encounter *before* they encounter them, so they feel prepared to succeed. It's important to remember that while the content of experiences changes, the process for a specific child generally remains the same. If you practice the process of their experience – how they typically think, how they typically respond, what they typically feel – then they can take that experiential template and use it in lots of different situations.

A common new experience for children is moving up one level on an athletic team. It requires a child to apply higher-level skills than he has used until now. Let's consider the practice that needs to take place when your child is about to play on this new team and is feeling insecure or anxious about it. How do you help him overcome his anxiety about playing for the first time with older children? What words do you hand your child so that he can manage the experience? Here's an example of how that would work:

A Practice Scenario: *"So you're the new kid on the team..."*

It is the night before the upcoming sporting event. Your children are 8 and 10. Your older child played on the team last year and is excited about the upcoming event. But your younger one has just moved up to a higher age group and has some anxiety about playing with the bigger children.

You have already taken steps to alleviate anxiety by planning for the event, and tomorrow you will be bringing along all that is needed so your younger child feels well prepared in regard to equipment, clothes, etc. You also want him to feel well prepared for taking his "big step" onto the playing field.

Your task is to practice the experience with your child: What will it be like to play with older children? If your child is anxious, what will he say to the coach? What will he say to the other kids? What will he actually do on the playing field?

Step #1: Provide your child the opportunity to talk about his fears, concerns or worries.

When you are an active listener, you are helping your child become a successful problem-solver. First, it is important to learn what your child is thinking that leads him to be anxious. So be relaxed and just talk about it.

The night before: Talk with your child about what the sporting event is going to look like, where it's going to be held, who's going to be there, and what his role is going to be. Who's going to ask him to do what? How is he going to fulfill the expectations of the coach? Does he seem anxious or nervous? Ask him what makes him feel this way. Maybe it's embarrassment about not being as tall as the other kids. Maybe it's worry that he'll let his teammates down. Also, engage your older child to talk with your younger child about his own experiences last year on the team.

Step #2: Write, draw and spell it out.

Writing, drawing and coloring help children to explore concepts and feelings in a new way. As he shares with you, consider writing down his words and thoughts on the left-hand side of a piece of paper and his feelings about them on the right-hand side, so that you can identify all the things that might be making him feel anxious, scared, annoyed or embarrassed. This activity will allow you to address each of his concerns calmly and skillfully; it will help him feel he has the skills to cope with the upcoming event.

Step #3: Give your child the words and action to manage his anxiety.

Let's say you identify with him that one of his thoughts is that the coach is going to ask him to do something he can't do, and he's feeling anxious. Now you can talk with your son about the position he played last year and how well he did at that position. If soccer is the sport, as an example, review with him how he has learned how to block and kick. Practice the words he can use with the coach in order to be placed in a position where he feels he can model quality skills. Practice a dialogue with your child so that he can respond easily if the coach is not listening to him or is asking him to do something he does not feel skilled at. Model for him the words he can use in order to get his needs met. Practice with him what he will say or do. Talk with him about what he will not do, as well.

Parent-Child Role-Play

Parent: *"Joey, let's pretend we are at the field and you want to talk with the coach about playing soccer on the new team. How do you want to introduce yourself to the coach?"*

Joey: *"I'll say, 'Hi Coach, I'm Joey Bordellini.'"*

Parent: *"Excellent. Now you want to tell the coach that you are familiar with the position of forward and ask him if you can play that position the first day out. What will you say?"*

Joey: *"I'll say, 'Hey coach, since I'm new to the team, may I play forward since I am used to that position?'"*

Parent: *"Great Joey. Now what if the coach says he needs you to play center?"*

Joey: *"I'll say that I don't know how to do that."*

Parent: *"Will you ask the coach to give you one or two tips on playing that position?"*

Joey: *"No, I'll just tell him I can't do that."*

Parent: *"Joey, sometimes a coach is going to ask you to do something new. That is part of being on a team. Can you say, 'Coach can you give me a few pointers on being the center?'"*

Joey: *"I can do that, Mom, but what if I am horrible and the kids laugh at me?"*

Parent: *"OK, now we're talking about feeling embarrassed. Tell me what you will do if the kids tease you or laugh at you."*

Joey: *"I'll say, 'Get out of my face.'"*

Parent: *"Is there a better way to be a team player and still stand up for yourself?"*

Joey: *"Yeah, I can kick a goal and show them how good I am at that."*

Parent: *"That may be a better solution. Show them you have skills and that you are ready to learn a new position if that's what the team needs. Remember, your brother Curt is out there too and they respect Curt. You can always go stand next to him if you are feeling picked on. One part of learning a new position is practicing it. We'll be at the game to watch and when we get home we'll all practice together. You are a great kid and a team player. We'll all be in this together."*

What do we learn from this scenario?

It's normal for a child to be nervous in a new situation. Your role is to help him work through his anxiety so that he can feel skillful. When you practice the words and even role-play in the backyard, in bed or in the car, you are fueling him with words and actions to handle the situation. If a child has the words and actions to cope with an anxiety-provoking experience, he will have the skills to cope with the situation much better.

If you practice the beginning, middle and end of the sporting experience with your son, talking about what's going to happen and what kinds of thoughts and feelings he's going to have, then he can apply that in lots of different places. He can apply it when the teacher asks him to read in front of the class and he feels like he doesn't read well. So, instead of having a fit, a meltdown or a depressive experience, your child can know he has some words and behavioral choices that he can apply *across* situations. Even if he does become upset by the experience as it happens, he will be much better situated to understand those feelings and process them effectively.

&

Prevention

Put prevention into play

I define prevention as the series of steps you take to teach your child how to avoid a negative experience such as a meltdown, an anxiety attack or a moment of extreme disappointment. Prevention includes knowing each of your individual children well enough to anticipate challenges and skill deficits before they arise.

As a point of observation, many of us are afraid to let our children experience a broad range of feelings in life. We try to protect our children from sadness, anger or disappointment. These feelings are part of the human experience. In a way, they propel and define our successes in life. Therefore, I believe that parenting is not about protecting your children from life experiences. Parenting is giving your children the words, actions, thoughts and behaviors to metabolize their experiences.

When implementing prevention strategies it is helpful to consider:

✦ Under what circumstances does my child do best?

✦ Under what circumstances does my child thrive?

- What gets in the way of my child succeeding?
- What might I be doing that gets in the way of my child succeeding?
- What can I do to make circumstances optimal for success?

Beware of unintentional sabotage

You can make it a lot easier on yourself and your children if you don't fall into the trap of unintentionally sabotaging your good efforts. In a dictionary definition, an act of sabotage is considered an intentional interfering with a desired outcome. But for our purposes, sabotage is a series of unintentional errors that get in the way of your effectiveness as a parent. An example of this would be trying to limit sugar and then filling your pantry with cookies and candy.

I want you to be vigilant so that you give your child every chance to succeed. Be aware of those little things that can send the wrong message to your child and interfere with your desired outcome. Remember, the aim here is to climb into proactive parenting and out of damage control by planning, preparing, practicing and preventing the challenges that affect your family's happiness.

Look closer

It is best to consider each discrete behavior you hope your child will exhibit and what is in the way of your child's achieving this behavior. OK, that seems like a tall order, but it's simple once you learn to work your observation muscles a bit. When your efforts at prevention do not appear to be working, take a step back and look closely at what is going on. Observation leads to a better understanding of what poses difficulties for your child. Then you can put in place some strategies to better equip your child for success.

A really important concept I teach parents is the difference between behavior that stems from a child's skill deficit and behavior that is from willful non-compliance. A later chapter will be devoted entirely to these two topics, but right now, we'll be focusing on identifying skill deficits.

Is this a skill deficit or willful non-compliance?

Let's give The Family Coach Method definition for these two terms:

The Family Coach Method Definition: **Skill Deficit**

(n.) With a skill deficit you are dealing with a *child's inability* to exhibit the expected behavior in this timeframe and under these circumstances.

*   *   *

The Family Coach Method Definition: **Willful Non-compliance**

(n.) With willful non-compliance you are dealing with a child who possesses a necessary skill set, yet obstinately and deliberately *chooses* not to exhibit behaviors required within a specific social, work, cultural, academic or family setting

---

Next, let's see what that means in the real world where you and your child live:

> ### How to Identify a Skill Deficit
> *(the short version)*
>
> Ask yourself these two questions:
> + What is the expected behavior?
>
> *and*
>
> + Can he/she do it?
>   (If yes, expect it. If no, teach it.)

Many times we ask our children to exhibit behaviors for which they have not yet developed the skills. The process of examining your child's ability to "do it" helps you to make sure you are fostering reasonable expectations of your child.

For Your Toolbox: *"Can He/She Do It?"*

This is an effective evaluation tool I use in my office and you can do at home. It works like this: Write down a specific behavior your child has had difficulty with in the past 48 hours. We'll call this "the expected behavior." Then, before enlisting your normal compliance strategies, ask yourself if your child possesses the skills necessary to complete the desired behavior. If the answer is yes, then expect it. If the answer is *no*, then teach it. It's that easy.

Now, let's look at some specific behavioral challenges.

BEHAVIOR 1: Sharing Toys

Step #1: What is the expected behavior?

"I expect my 5-year-old daughter to share her toys with her brother."

Step #2: Can she do it?

Here are the kinds of things to look at as you consider the answer:

✦ Did I discretely define one behavior I am seeking my child to exhibit?

✦ Does my child have the requisite skills to exhibit this behavior?

✦ Are there any roadblocks that inhibit my child's ability to exhibit the behavior? For example, did my child sleep well and eat well?

✦ Have I defined which toys are for sharing and which are personal and will not be played with by others?

✦ Have I told my child she may place special toys in a basket in her closet and those will be just her own, no sharing?

✦ If my child will share another toy, but not the requested toy, did I offer that alternative solution for the children?

Step #3: If yes, expect it.

If you determine that your child has the skills for the expected behavior, then expect it! You can ensure the behavior by clarifying expectations and establishing a time frame for sharing. It might look like this:

Parent: *"Shiloh, James has asked to play your Nintendo. That is a toy we agreed we would share right now. You now have ten seconds to hand the toy to your brother."*

Step #4: If no, teach it.

If you determine that your child does not yet have the skills for the expected behavior, then teach it. Help the child to choose an alternate toy. Your child now has an opportunity to model sharing and practice sharing.

Parent: *"Shiloh, James has asked to play your Nintendo. When will you be willing to let him play? In five minutes or in ten minutes?"*

BEHAVIOR 2: Reading

Step #1: What is the expected behavior?

"I expect my 7-year-old son to read for twenty minutes each night."

Step #2: Can he do it?

✦ Did I discretely define one behavior I am seeking my child to exhibit?

✦ Does my child have the requisite skills to exhibit this behavior?

✦ Are there any roadblocks that inhibit my child's ability to exhibit the behavior? For example, did my child sleep well and eat well?

✦ Does my child know how to read?

✦ Can my child articulate phonemes?

✦ Is the book at my child's level?

✦ Have I read this book with the child before?

✦ Might I read to my child first, then ask him to read to me?

Step #3: If yes, expect it.

Set a timer for 20 minutes, establish a comfortable reading area, and check in with your child to make sure he is getting closer to his goals.

Step #4: If no, teach it.

Read with your child. Help him with his phonics or secure a booklist from his teacher of age-appropriate books on your child's reading level. Perhaps your child will need to work up to 20 minutes, or he needs to read along with you at first.

Parenting Mindfully

It is valuable to ask yourself, "Does the child have the skills to exhibit the behavioral expectation?" Sometimes what we believe is willful non-compliance is actually fatigue, stress or a skill deficit. Parenting mindfully includes having the presence of mind to realistically assess what is willful disobedience and what might be a skill deficit or *situational* non-compliance due to hunger, fatigue, or expectations that are above your child's skill level.

SITUATIONAL NON-COMPLIANCE
(Just think of it as PMS for kids,
except that it can happen anytime)

Sometimes your child can look like he is exhibiting willful non-compliance but he is not. These are times when a child is resistant, and it is just because circumstances are making it harder than usual for him to behave as expected. If you consider your own behavior, sometimes you experience situational noncompliance as well – you're underfed, and overtired, or you just haven't had enough down time. We all deal with it. And it's the same for kids. For example, when your child is tired and has not eaten, he may be more grumpy than normal.   All it takes is a cup of milk or a little turkey and cheese to get him back on track.

You, The Skilled Observer

Right now, I want to show you how to hone a very important skill of your own. This is the key skill you will need to develop to make Planning, Preparation, Practice and Prevention truly effective: **Observation**. Have I got a tool for you!

For Your Toolbox: *The ABC Detective Kit*

As a caring, involved parent you're constantly developing new skills, including the ability to recognize problems in your child's life and ferret out the causes. That's what the rest of this chapter is going to be about: training yourself to be a first class observer, a skilled detective. This isn't about spying on your children; it's about systematically tracking down clues to behaviors that seem to defy explanation and easy solutions.

How to Become a Behavioral Detective

Before I ever teach a family about a direct behavioral intervention, I always teach them how to become detectives and start to observe their children's lives more closely. The most valuable thing you can do is to identify the specific behavior that is a challenge, then call on your observational skills in order to better understand the behavior — before you intervene. This is "being a behavioral detective." It makes life a lot easier by helping you recognize when it's really time to intervene.

The Family Coach Definition: **Intervention**

(n.) A corrective action taken, after appropriate evaluation and careful consideration, to address a child's (or parent's) behavior and/or skill deficit.

If you intervene too soon without full understanding of the situation, you might be implementing *ready, fire, aim* instead of *ready, aim, fire*. If you fire before you aim, chances are you're going to miss the mark and need to re-do the intervention. You may also have to undo your mistakes surrounding the initial misfire. Don't worry – you're not going to do irreparable harm if you don't get it right at first. Just like with your kids, practice will quickly improve your own skills, too.

When I work with parents, we first talk together about how we can collect data, make decisions and identify the appropriate intervention. The data collection can include everything from looking at a child's temperament, to possible diagnoses, to exploring executive function deficits (i.e., the cognitive skills that regulate behaviors – like the inability to anticipate outcomes or adapt to changing situations).

This helps us learn a lot about what leads up to a behavior, what maintains it and what could shift it to a new more productive habit or behavior. You can do this by drawing on a big sheet like I do, or writing in a journal where you examine behaviors over time. You can describe, elaborate and explore behaviors in detail. I encourage you to set up the easy-reference journal template below. It will be an invaluable help to you for your sleuthing activities.

Setting Up Your ABC Detective Journal

Thirty minutes from now you'll have a wonderful tool at your disposal, ready to go. Here's a brief overview of how to lay out the pages of the journal (or graph pages or individual sheets, if you prefer). At the end of this chapter we lay out a sample detective journal page for you to review.

The detective journal has 5 columns.

Across the top of the page define the behavior. This describes the specific observed behavior.

✦ The first column is labeled Date/Time - This marks the date and time the observed behavior took place.

✦ The next three columns are A,B,C – described below.

✦ The fifth column is for Notes. This is where you can reflect on what you observe.

Yours could look something like this:

Behavior: (Who did what)

Date/Time	A	B	C	Notes

Some sample behaviors include:

+ Keisha could not get out of bed this morning.
+ Leslie would not stop picking on her younger sister.
+ James bit a child in preschool.
+ Alison refused to eat her dinner.
+ Sarah would not share her toys with a playmate.
+ Tyrone refused to do his nightly reading.
+ Jamison swore at his dad.

Here is a description of columns A, B and C.

Column A

This records what leads up to the behavior, what's going on at the time, who's present at the time, and what are the circumstances prior to the behavior. Your notes in this column address questions like:

+ Has my child eaten well?
+ Has my child slept well?
+ Did he have his cuddly with him or something to help soothe him during a transition?
+ Was he prepared for the requested behavior or personal experience?
+ Did my child sleep enough?
+ Did he have a late-afternoon snack?
+ Was I impatient and hence contributed to the misbehavior?

✦ Were there too many children in the classroom this morning, so that the class was loud or unruly?

✦ Was my child woken up too early?

✦ Was there an adult present to help the child with a skill deficit? Did he have the necessary skills to manage the experience?

Column B

This records the details of the actual behavior, its length, duration and severity:

✦ What happened?

  What behavior was exhibited?

  How long did it go on for?

✦ How severe was the behavior?

Column C

This describes the outcome and consequences of the behavior.

✦ Who was there?

✦ Who was involved?

✦ What did each person say?

  What did each person do?

  What happened next?

  Were consequences employed?

  Was discipline used?

✦ What form of discipline?

  How was it administered?

  By whom?

  How did my child respond?

  What seemed to work well?

  What did not work well?

  What improvements might be needed?

Stop, Look and Listen

See how this works? Now, the next time your child misbehaves, you have the template all set up to help you with your behavioral detective skills. Sit back and observe. Take notes. Consider what you said and did. Consider what your child said and did. Consider what others said and did. Just being aware will likely alter your behavior as well as the behavior of your child.

You'll be amazed by what you learn by simply looking and listening in this new, highly focused way. When you understand the *who, what, when, where* and *how* of your child's behavior you can make more informed choices regarding how to intervene.

In the next section, we'll see how your behavioral observation abilities will help you to effectively Plan, Prepare, Practice and Prevent.

Using Your ABC Detective Tool

 Let's imagine that we have a 6-year-old boy named Sammy who cries every day when his dad brings him to school. Sammy has separation difficulty from his dad. This is painful for both Sammy and Dad.

The crying usually lasts about 45 minutes before Sammy can calm himself down and begin to participate in his day. So Dad, having recently acquired his ABC detective tool, decides it's time to get to the bottom of the behavior. The problem is clear-cut: crying when Daddy leaves Sammy at school. Dad now begins his observations in earnest.

Day one: Sammy starts to cry in the car. Dad has to peel him out of the car and carry him to the classroom, where he offers him into the arms of a caring teacher and tries to soothe him for about ten minutes. But Sammy's crying just escalates. Eventually, with a lot of anxiety, sadness and even frustration, Dad pulls himself away and goes home. When he gets home, he takes out his ABC journal or marker board and writes about what just happened...in detail.

Experience: (at the top of the page)

Sammy cried when I left him at school. He does this every day.

Column A: (what leads up to the behavior) *I could not get Sammy out of the car so I lifted him up and carried him in. Sammy had woken up early and had refused most of his breakfast. He was irritable and clingy. He did not want to go to school.*

Column B: (the behavior itself) *Sammy clung to me and cried when I brought him into the classroom. He refused to go with his teacher. I sat down to help him calm himself, which made things worse.*

Column C: (outcome) *Eventually, I peeled Sammy off me. I was tired and sad and frustrated. The teacher held Sammy's hand and I left the classroom while he screamed and cried.*

Throughout the week: Mom and Dad – maybe also teacher, and eventually son – talk about what happens each day and they write it down. They notice a few things after a few days. One is that Sammy doesn't eat well in the morning.

He's not really hungry and eats only a few spoonfuls of cereal in the morning. Sammy goes to school at 9:00 AM and he doesn't have a snack until 10:30 AM.

His teacher is caring, but seems to be a bit of a remote traditionalist who doesn't believe in coddling children. She expects Sammy to calm himself.

Sammy's parents wonder if he doesn't receive much nurturing, guidance or skill-building during the 45-minute crying episode.

Despite attempts to calm him down, he doesn't get any better.

Solving the Case
(with the help of Plan, Prepare, Practice and Prevent)

Because of their behavioral observations, and because they've played behavioral detective, Mom and Dad are able to step away from the emotionally charged situation and, armed with an effective tool, become neutral observers.

Now that they have the big picture of what's going on, they are ready to plan.

Making the Plan

Mom and Dad talk, with each other and with other friends and family members, about their experiences with children, and what they've done in similar situations. They note that there are actually many points of intervention that the family can try on their own and encourage the teacher to try as well. They generate a plan that Dad's going to introduce to the teacher.

The Preparation

Nutrition: Mom and Dad decide that they will prepare Sammy for each day, starting with a good, high-protein breakfast: First, they're going to swap sugar and carbohydrates in the morning for a few tablespoons of protein. This will sustain Sammy's body and brain for the first hour or hour and a half of school. They make a little menu for him to choose from and simply say, "Each day you can choose off the menu and Mommy or Daddy will sit down with you and have breakfast. We'll all enjoy a little brain food together before we go to school." They put things on the list, like organic chicken mixed with brown rice with teriyaki sauce, turkey chili, Swiss cheese and egg scramble, cottage-cheese on celery, hummus with turkey, and cheese on a mini bagel and Italian meatballs.

So now Sammy's breakfast list is full of super solid food, which can sustain him a lot longer than cereal with milk, especially since he's a finicky eater and only wants to eats two or three ounces at a time. Mom and Dad decide that on days when he doesn't want to eat at all, they can give him three to six ounces of a quality protein shake.

Preparing Sammy for the Handoff at School: The parents divide the process into three steps: 1) driving to school, 2) entering the classroom, and 3) kissing Daddy so-long.

Step #1 of going to school includes: getting his lunch, shoes, and backpack; getting into the car; driving to school while singing songs or talking with Dad or imagining one fun thing that will happen at school that day. (Remember rhythm, routines and rituals from Chapter 3? Here's a good example of this in action.)

Step #2 is getting out of the car, entering the classroom and participating in the early morning organizational activities of the classroom. At this point, Sammy's dad is still on the scene.

Step #3 is saying goodbye to Daddy, giving him a kiss and a hug, and telling him you'll see him this afternoon after school.

Practicing with Sammy Beforehand

With this routine in mind, Mom, Dad and Sammy sit down at the table and Mom and Dad talk about what Sammy can expect will happen every morning from now on, and what they expect of him. This is their opportunity to practice the next day's events with Sammy, address his anxieties or worries, and reinforce his skills.

Together they create a story about "Sammy the Successful School Warrior" – and Dad writes it down on a big sheet of paper (Of course! They are dedicated Family Coach scribblers). It's a very simple story, with a beginning, middle and end that elaborates the three components of success: getting into the car in a prepared way, getting out of the car and entering school, then beginning to get engaged in the classroom and saying goodbye to Daddy.

"Bridging" for Success

Sammy's parents share their strategy with the teacher. Dad suggests that each day when Sammy comes to school, he shows his teacher an art project that he made at home. This art project creates a bridge between the parents and the teacher. Sammy is excited about sharing his project and is reinforced by the personal attention he gets from his teacher at the time of transition. The parents have asked the teacher to let Sammy make an art project to bring home from school, and the teacher agrees. Another bridge.

The Family Coach Definition: **The Bridge**

(n.) A bridge is anything offered between two people that serves as a window to the next opportunity, task or experience. A bridge can be handing the teacher your child's blanket so that he has it to comfort him at school. It can be an appetizer you bring to a party that says you are dedicated to making the evening an enjoyable shared experience. It can be a hug you offer your child when she gets home to say, "You made it through the day. Now come in, let's have soup and share our love." This is an important concept parents use in everyday life all the time, but rarely do they take full advantage its power.

How is Sammy doing today?

Sammy is now better fed and experiences a family breakfast before school. In the car he gets to hold his art project to share with the teacher. While he would still prefer to stay home with his dad, he is armed with more skills to manage the transition from home to school. He still cries when his dad leaves, but within a few days his crying episodes became shorter. He is able to engage more at school because his teacher now lets him sit down to make an art project to bring home to his parents. The experience moves from an unhappy routine of loss to one of sharing, nurturance and age-appropriate skill development.

That's an example of how one can use the behavioral detective process to better understand a situation in order to generate some commonsense intervention strategies.

A Note About Brain Food

One of Sammy's issues was that he was not eating a balanced diet each morning. Too often parents overlook this most important prevention tool. Discussions about feeding our children whole food abound these days. I am pleased by this. Many educators, dietitians and psychologists are sounding the alarm about the overuse of quick, overly processed convenience foods in our children's diets. It's no secret that our children's health is declining. This not only sets them up for health problems later in life, it can directly affect their energy, attention level and moods. Nutrition is an important and complicated topic. If you have any questions or concerns about your family's diet, don't hesitate to bring it up with your physician. Here are a few interesting and informative books on the subject: *Nourishing Hope*, by Julie Matthews; *The Ultramind Solution*, by Mark Hyman, MD; *The Eat Clean Diet*, by Tosca Reno.

A little creativity goes a long way

In addition to the planning and preparing, Sammy's family used some creative forms of practice as well. They made a story about "going to school." There are as many variations on this as there are parents and kids. You can be as creative as you want, as formal or as free form, as long as it speaks to your child. You could go so far as to set up a little schoolroom in your home and go through your morning routines. You can practice on a consistent basis for a few days or months and change it up over time: Involve stuffed animals, involve brothers and sisters, involve the family dog.

Is it worth it? Oh, yeah!

The key is to expose your children to situations so they can feel masterful and skillful when they have to do something they don't like, that causes anxiety, or when they have to adapt to new situations. If it seems like a lot of work, think about it as an upfront expenditure that will pay off quickly over time as your mornings, evenings or bed-times become predictable and efficient.

Now, when we get back to the concept of planning, preparing, practicing and preventing, you can see that being a behavioral detective gives you the ability to step back and look at the bigger picture first. It helps you move from a cycle of loss that is not working, and into a pattern of rhythm, routine, relationship and sharing that helps the children to develop a new set of skills. With all these interventions, you're not just bringing your child to school, kissing him and saying "see you after school"; you are arming him with a series of expected behaviors. Once they are familiar to him, he is more in control of the transition.

A system of planning, preparing, practicing and preventing is the most effective way to begin to modify a behavior or develop a skill where a skill doesn't exist. It all comes down to Observation. And it's the beginning of the end of living in damage control mode. Oh, happy day!

SUMMARY

When you begin to implement planning, preparing, practicing and prevention into your family life, you are setting your children up for success by giving them tools to meet life's challenges. In the next chapter, we will build on the foundation of skill-development, we will discover strategies that allow your children to further use these new skills – and we will help your little ones to develop a relationship with the "R" word: Responsibility.

HANDS-ON WITH THE FAMILY COACH

ACTIVITY #1

Create Your ABC Journal: Be a Detective

If you take the time to create your own ABC Journal, I assure you it will help you to better understand your child's behavior within 24-48 hours. I find the clearest way to keep track of a behavior pattern is to set up a behavior chart in your ABC Journal, if you prefer, on a separate sheet of plain or graph paper.

Either way, this is your journal, write it, review it, color it, edit it and keep it the way you wish. My hope is that you will give it a try.

As noted earlier, you can write the behavior across the top of the page.

In the first column write "Date/Time." It is helpful to look at any patterns regarding when the transgression takes place. Then label the A, B and C columns. As a reminder, here's what each column will record:

Column A: (what leads up to the behavior)

Column B: (details of the behavior itself)

Column C: (outcome)

You might add a Note column as well.

BEHAVIOR: *Amy kicked Sarah*

Date/ Time	A	B	C	Note
Sunday Sept. 20, 2009 8:45 pm	We were ready to read then turn the lights out as part of our evening routine. Jack was ready to tuck Amy in, I was ready to tuck Sarah in. They were told to each get a book from the bookshelf.	Sarah grabbed the book Amy wanted from the shelf. Amy kicked Sarah. Sarah screamed. Jack went running to see what had happened.	We made both girls sit down immediately. Each child got to tell her story one at a time. We told the girls that each of them had broken a family rule. They were given the chance to apologize and show they could calm down. The girls had to role-play how they could have made better choices. Bedtime was set to 15 minutes earlier the next night. Sarah went to sleep crying.	We set the girls up by letting them stay up too late. We were kind but firm about no violence. Will help the girls wind down earlier.

ACTIVITY #2

❧

The "Look, Listen and Learn" Game
(Building observation skills)

Observation is a powerful skill. Being observant lets you evaluate with skillfulness your environment, the people in it, and the actions others take. Children with poor observation skills often find themselves in trouble at home and at school. Teaching your children how to be keen observers is a gift they will use for a lifetime.

Here's a simple game you can play with your children anywhere (except maybe in church or at the movies). It's a little like Where's Waldo? in real life. When you are at the park playing, or in the bagel store ordering breakfast, use your powers of observation with your children by saying,

"Let's play Look, Listen and Learn."

"I see a baker making bagels," your child might say.

Then you might add, *"I see a woman in a bright red sweater walking to a table."*

Then your child adds, with more words and a more detailed observation, *"I see three kids sitting at the table waiting for the woman."*

You can practice wondering aloud (but not too loud) who the people are, what they are doing, what are they eating, etc. This is a fun non-judgmental way to become a keen observer in the world. As your children's skills become more developed, you can discuss the meaning of people's behavior and why they do what they do.

III

Manage behaviors with Freedom and Consequenceland

CHAPTER 6

SET BOUNDARIES AND LIMITS

❦

Have you ever had anyone tell you, "You need to set boundaries with your child," or, "You have no boundaries"? Did you look at them, puzzled? What do they mean? What is a boundary, really, when we're talking about our own kids?

The Family Coach Method Definition: **Boundary**

(n.) An emotional, psychological, or physical line that defines a space along the edge of a person, place or thing.

Boundaries are one of the most important concepts you will teach your children in their early years. If you have children, you have already taught them about boundaries, perhaps without even knowing it.

In the first few weeks of life, baby is without boundaries. From baby's perspective you and baby are one. As baby climbs up on your chest to nurse or lies comfortably in your arms, baby knows you and herself as one. As your baby's developmental skills grow she begins to experience that you and she are distinct. She experiences needing you to care for her basic needs and she yelps, cries and wiggles to get closer to you. This is the beginning of baby's understanding of inter-personal boundaries – when she is hungry and she calls out to you to feed her, she experiences the distinctness between you and her.

You may have no memory of it, but when you were a baby there came a time when you began to experience that you and your caregiver or parent were distinct beings and then you tried to stay physically closer to get your needs met.

As your child grows you teach her about her own personal boundaries, the boundaries she needs to observe within her social relationships and the boundaries she defines around her own thoughts, actions and feelings.

Boundaries help your child succeed as a social being.

Boundaries are protective, pro-social and proactive. Children with "good boundaries" know how to:

> get help from Mommy when they cannot do something themselves
>
> wait for Daddy to finish dinner before they expect to go outside and play
>
> close the door when they use the bathroom
>
> follow the playground rules
>
> sit where they are told to on the circle-time carpet
>
> stay in their rooms during rest time
>
> enter into and exit from social interactions with friends
>
> respect the space of a schoolmate
>
> kindly ask for something he needs
>
> move over on the bench so that another child can sit down

I could go on and on. When children understand healthy boundaries they are really ahead of the game in childhood.

Defining a Boundary

OK, let's get a little more detailed here. In The Family Coach Method, there are three distinct types of boundaries in your relationships with your children:

1. The interpersonal boundary

2. The space between, and

3. The space within.

Now, don't glaze over – this isn't complicated; in fact, it is super interesting.

The Interpersonal Boundary

The interpersonal boundary is essentially where you end and another person begins. You set interpersonal boundaries with your children in physical space. When you step in front of your child so that he does not touch the ornaments on the Christmas tree, you are setting a boundary. When you tell your child, "Don't touch the light socket," you are establishing a boundary. This boundary has to do with physical space and your child's actions within it.

The interpersonal boundary can also be emotional. Your emotional boundaries define the space in which you experience psychological comfort. When you speak to your child in a demeaning or sarcastic tone, you are not respecting their interpersonal boundaries.

Boundaries in general are defined by your personal rules of living.

The interpersonal boundary defines who can touch you physically, where, when and how. I like to think of boundaries as concentric circles of intimacy. Your interpersonal boundary likely begins with a small circle in which your most intimate relationships are housed. The boundary then expands depending on circumstances, with several concentric circles that you allow people to enter and exit.

The Interpersonal Boundary is where ...

+ you teach your children where one person ends and another person begins.
+ you teach your children about personal space.
+ you teach your children about physical space.
+ you teach your children that their feelings matter.

✦ you teach your children that another person is not to use a demeaning or sarcastic tone with them.

The Day Samantha Set a Boundary

Let's talk for a moment about Samantha. Samantha is the mother of 3 children ages 6, 4 and 2. When I first met Sam, as she likes to be called, she was overwhelmed by the daily management of her children. They were always climbing on her, tugging on her and incessantly needing her. When I first entered Sam's home, she was holding two children and her 6-year-old boy was grabbing her skirt as she ushered me in, exasperated. "Mommy, I'm hungry!" he cried. We all tumbled over one another as we bounded for the kitchen to feed Johnny.

As Samantha balanced the two little ones, while reaching in the fridge for some turkey and cheese, I took Johnny's hand and walked him to the kitchen table. I told Johnny that when he sat in his chair at the kitchen table his mommy would bring him a bite to eat. Johnny sat willingly and quietly, to Samantha's amazement. Next was the 4-year-old, an articulate boy with an enormous smile. "Smiley," I said, "where is your seat?" He just looked at me. I helped him hop into a seat and said, "Voilá, your new seat!" He smiled.

Samantha's children had never been told they each had a home base at the kitchen table. Once they had a home, they knew where to go to wait for their needs to be met. From now on, when Samantha was feeling smothered by her children, she had a "start here" spot to take the children to in order to begin whatever task needed to be accomplished. In a matter of minutes the children learned about boundaries. They also experienced that there is a space between two people and that if they were going to get their needs met they had to be sitting in their "home base."

Simple, right? All you need is a table and chairs; I bet you have some in your home. You might even have placemats you can use to define each child's space. Kids love to know where their place is. Adults just forget that it often comes down to the simple things.

When, from a young age, you gently teach your child that there are emotional and physical boundaries in their relationships, you empower them to have healthy relationships.

The Space Between

As your child grows she begins to experience *the space between you* as a place to work, love, share and grow. As you sit on the floor to play or hold her hand walking to the 'fridge for juice, she experiences the space between you as a place of comfort and security. The Space Between boundary marks the emotional and physical space between you and another person. If you are thinking in pictures, the space between is the white space. It is open and empty.

I think of the space between as a "working space" where problems are solved, solutions are generated, and skills are built. The space between is where you exchange knowledge, warmth and understanding as you "work" with your children to teach them skills such as feeling identification, mood modulation, mood management and relationship management. It is also where you counsel, teach and guide your children or loved ones on their sibling relationships, peer relationships, social behaviors and developmental experiences.

The Day Harmony Cried in the Space Between

One day after school, Kevin picked up his daughter Harmony at preschool, only to be rushed at the door by a sobbing child.

"Harmony, what is it?" Kevin asked, alarmed.

"Miss Jane says I can't bring blankie anymore 'cause I am a big girl."

"Come here and let's sit down and talk about this," her father said as he led her to a spot beneath an old elm in the school's front yard.

He and Harmony sat beneath the tree, Harmony rubbing her eyes and Kevin inquiring as to the fate of blankie. He comforted his daughter while they talked about how she would manage her feelings in school without the presence of her beloved blankie. It was in the space between that they discussed and addressed Harmony's feelings about going to school and leaving blankie at home.

When your child faces a task demand such as the first day of school, a loss on the soccer field or a conflict with a peer, the space between is where you and the child navigate strategies to cope with new experiences, build new skills and practice skill implementation.

The Space Between is where...

- ✦ you take the time to get to know your child better
- ✦ you help your child to better understand the beginning, middle and end of her actions
- ✦ you teach your child the words, feelings and actions to better manage life experiences
- ✦ you listen, reflect, hear and respond with warmth
- ✦ you build the relationship...so do not rush to solve, shame or ridicule your child. Be reflective, talk slowly and take this opportunity to listen carefully to your child.
- ✦ you express empathy: "You are having so much fun on the scooter, you'd rather not give someone else a turn" "It's hard to go to school when you are worried the kids will tease you" "Sometimes you wish your dad would spend special time just with you."
- ✦ your relationship grows as you show love, affection, patience, caring and empathy.

The Line of Demarcation

The **line of demarcation** usually refers to a boundary that sets a limit, most often on behavior. We reviewed rules extensively in Chapters 1 and 2. When you establish rules and limits for your children in your own home, these are lines of demarcation. When you indicate that your children need to complete their morning routines before they can watch television, that is a line of demarcation. When you indicate that your children are to sit at the dinner table until everyone is done, that is a line of demarcation. When you communicate that your children are to treat one another with respect and physical kindness, that is a line of demarcation. The line of demarcation is a critical boundary that you set so that your children learn your family's expected behaviors.

The Space Within

The Space Within boundary is the area within yourself where you define your value-based rules for emotional and physical health. Helping your children know where their own internal boundaries exist is very important. For one child, the critical glance or mean tone of another person might feel quite hurtful. That tells you that, for him, an internal boundary has been crossed.

For another child, a sibling asking about why she peed in bed might feel hurtful. That too reveals a boundary. For yet a third child, experiencing the shame of being "caught" by a parent while dancing with abandon might indicate that there's a particular boundary for that child. Some kids are shy and need a lot of personal space.

Some children feel very strongly about their own bodily boundaries and they do not wish for others to see or hear them poop, pee or fart. Don't laugh; OK, laugh for a second, then gather yourself and respect that even very young children have internal boundaries. The earlier you recognize and respect them the healthier your relationship with your young child will be.

Got Boundaries?

You have internal boundaries too. In order to be truly effective at respecting your children's boundaries, it helps to be cognizant of where yours are. People often focus on setting interpersonal boundaries before they have defined their own personal boundaries.

Let me say it again: People often focus on setting interpersonal boundaries before they have defined their own personal boundaries. Stop, right here. Have you defined your own boundaries? Before you can begin to define your rules for interacting with others, you need to know how you define the rules for yourself and your own personal boundaries.

Jason and His Space Within

At 8 years of age, Jason was beginning to define his own comfort level in his emotional relationships with others. Jason's sport of choice was diving. When many of the other children were playing team sports such as baseball and football, Jason was often at the pool with his diving coach. One day Jason said to his dad, "Matthew says I'm a wimp 'cause I dive and I don't play football." Jason's dad asked how that made Jason feel. Jason said, "Bad. Should I play football instead?"

Jason's dad told him the following, "Jason we all have our own likes and dislikes. Whether you like chess or dance or diving, that is up to you. Let's practice some things you can say when the kids tease you, because it is how *you* feel and what *you* like that matters." Jason's dad was teaching his son that his feelings were important. While others might form opinions about his chosen sport, it was up to Jason to draw the lines and tell others that he liked diving and was proud of his accomplishments.

Why do children need boundaries?

Children need boundaries in order to feel safe, nurtured and loved. Whether a boundary is internal, related to our thoughts and feelings, or external, related to how we manage the space in our relationships, boundaries are central to our emotional and physical development.

There are many instances of external boundary-setting that are designed not only to maintain health and peace within a family, but also to help children develop internal self-control. It can help them establish expectations in their interpersonal relationships, and to be able to self-set behavioral boundaries based on the circumstances and norms of any given setting.

> ✔ **Example:** **A 5-year-old may be able to still sit on his parent's lap but he is also expected to remain in his seat in kindergarten.**
>
> **Another: When we teach our children to "use an indoor voice" and "monitor your tone," that external boundary might become so well internalized that a child will speak quietly in public and use a polite tone with teachers.**

Boundaries can change

Boundaries are not set in stone; they are "fluid" depending on children's development needs, ages and family circumstances. Boundaries may change over time as needs and circumstances change.

> ✔ **Example:** **The line of demarcation for the bedtime hour may be different during the school year versus summertime. During the school year the bedtime might be set at 8:00 pm, so that your children are well rested and prepared to thrive at school. In the summer, when school expectations are not relevant, the bedtime boundary might shift to 9:00 pm, when playing outside takes place until dark and wake-up is moved to a later time.**

Boundaries may also vary from child to child, as some children might need more external boundaries in order to define and manage their own internal boundaries. A child's internal boundaries may influence how they manage their internal feelings about going to bed on time, as well as what behaviors they choose to exhibit at any given time.

The Family Coach Method Definition: **Limits**

(n.) A limit signals the upper and lower boundaries of an action. Limits clarify the boundaries in which a child chooses to or chooses not to exhibit a range of behaviors. When we think of limits, we think of defining expected behaviors with upper and lower restrictions.

Limits are...

Limits are not to be confused with rules. Rules are the principles or assertions that customarily govern expected behaviors. Limits are the borders or lines that clarify rule violations.

Limits can be set around most behaviors including, but not limited to:

- ✦ Appropriate use of one's body with other people
- ✦ Appropriate use of words
- ✦ Choosing a healthy lunch
- ✦ Completing daily chores
- ✦ Completing homework in a timely manner
- ✦ Doing as a parent instructs
- ✦ Eating behaviors
- ✦ Following the rules
- ✦ Getting to school on time
- ✦ Maintaining safe behaviors
- ✦ Playing fairly
- ✦ Respecting the physical space of others

✦ Respecting toys and household items

✦ Returning the car at an appropriate time

✦ Taking turns

✦ Use of appropriate language

There are many purposes for setting limits, such as:

✦ To define expected behavior clearly

✦ To keep children safe

✦ To assist children in socialization and friendship behaviors

✦ To secure parent-child cooperation without conflicts and power struggles

✦ To teach rules in the clearest and most understandable way

✦ To stop misbehavior with natural and logical consequences

✦ To teach children to solve problems on their own

✦ To teach independence, accountability and responsibility in one's behavior

When setting a limit consider:

✦ What is the expected behavior?

✦ Have you clearly defined the behavior?

✦ Has an opportunity to exhibit the appropriate behavior been provided?

✦ Have you clearly demarcated the range of acceptable behaviors?

✦ Have time frames for the expected behavior been established?

✦ Have you communicated the outcome of compliance?

✦ Have you communicated the outcome for non-compliance?

✦ Have the consequences for non-compliance been determined collaboratively?

✦ Are the parents consistent in their approach to the expected behavior each time?

Establishing, Implementing, and Reinforcing Limits

Establishing, implementing, and reinforcing limits is one of the most crucial aspects of parenting. You must know what the limit for a specific behavior is and be prepared to teach your children how to observe the limit. While limits shift over time based on the developmental and behavioral needs of your children, at any given moment you must be able to set appropriate limits and then *be consistent* in implementing and reinforcing them. There are four guidelines for establishing, implementing and reinforcing a limit. You must:

- ✦ Know that your child possesses the skill to observe the limit
- ✦ Clearly communicate the limit
- ✦ Be consistent in setting the limit
- ✦ Be consistent in responding to limit violations when they occur

We have extensively reviewed identifying whether or not your child has the skills to exhibit an expected behavior. Remember, if you set a limit on a behavior, make sure your child has the skills to observe the limit.

Defining Limits by Age Group
(not one-size-fits-all, but pretty close)

3-Year-Olds and Limits:
You are now living in the social world

Typical limits set for children up to 3 years of age revolve around safety and socialization.

> **What a child may touch:** A toddler or young child is likely safe touching their own toys, child-friendly utensils, socialized family pets, their own clothing and safe household items such as furniture, their car seats, their books, etc.

What a child may not touch: A toddler or young child must not touch electrical outlets, sharp objects, unfamiliar animals, breakable objects and dangerous household items such as cords on window shades, etc.

What a child may do with his or her body: A toddler or young child is encouraged to respect his body and the bodies of others. He may hug, kiss, cuddle, walk, run, jump and play with appropriate toys or household objects such as plastic kitchen utensils.

What a child may not do with his or her body: A toddler or young child may not hit, push or scratch others. She may not throw items that are not intended to be thrown. She may not throw her body recklessly on the floor, bang her head against the wall or crib, or exhibit behaviors that can lead to self-harm. She may not climb on household furniture or leave the immediate care of her parents when out in public.

4- to 6-Year-Olds and Limits:
Do this, but don't do that

Typical limits set for children between 4 and 6 years of age revolve around safety, health, rule compliance, learning and socialization.

What a child may do and may not do in the realm of safety and health: With their growing independence, early school-agers enjoy modeling their competence. However, there are certain skills that they still need help with in order to stay safe and healthy – such as riding in car seats, accompanied swimming and using household tools and implements.

When and how a child follows the rules established by authority figures: A significant part of preschool to first grade is learning how to follow the rules. It can be a difficult transition from nurturance to socialized behavior. Once the rules have been established, limits must be reinforced so the child knows "Do this, but don't do that."

What a child may and may not do in interactions with peers: When a child goes from a home environment to a group setting, be it daycare or a classroom sharing, the limits might involve waiting one's turn, participating in a group and following directions.

7- and 8-Year-Olds and Limits:
Using your skills to learn and grow

Typical limits set for children between 7 and 8 years of age revolve around safety, socialization, academic learning and rule compliance.

What a child may do and may not do in the realm of safety and health, independently: In grade school, issues of independence step up a notch. Children are away from their parents for longer periods of time. They visit the homes of friends, are left alone with other adults at sporting events, and have access to technology around which time and content limits must be set.

When and how a child follows the rules established by authority figures: The range and type of limit testing exhibited by a school-age child is broader than that of a younger child. School-agers are stronger, they use more powerful words, and their actions can actually hurt others emotionally and physically. Limits must be set around rules-following behavior so that children are compliant and well socialized.

How a child manages peer relationships: Peer relationships are central to school-agers. They have play dates, play on athletic teams, participate in hobbies, and work through conflicts such as those found in cliques and bullying. They require close observation and attention by parents to stay healthy, productive and safe.

As stated earlier, it is always best if a family or classroom has defined a culture for itself, "what kind of family we are" and "what we value," before creating rules for behavior and defining the upper and, when applicable, lower limits of a given behavior. Now that we have in mind the domains of limits commonly set in different age groups, let's explore establishing **limits around behavior**.

Using Boundaries and Limits to Teach Healthy Behavior

Learning the skills of healthy socialization is a central aspect of growing up in the preschool and school-aged years. Children need to understand boundaries and limits in order to be high functioning children at home and in school. While you are the first line of education regarding boundaries and limits, schools can do a lot for your child in teaching them how to join the social world of childhood.

Values at School

It is my hope that when your children are in school between the ages of 3 to 8, their classroom is teaching them about character, values-based behavior and the importance of making pro-social behavioral choices. When you visit a school you are considering for your children it is important that the school not only has a clear academic curriculum but also a social and emotional curriculum.

My friend, Dr. Michele Borba, is the mom of three sons and the author of *The Big Book of Parenting Solutions*. Michele has some helpful thoughts to contribute to the discussion of schools and how to know if one is right for your child:

How I'd Choose a Preschool

When my sons were small, I always chose their preschools based on one factor: I would visit the school and watch how the teachers interacted with the students. Did they treat the children with respect? Were they warm and caring? Did they discipline with dignity? And then I visualized my son in that setting. If I could see him as happy, secure and confident, then it was the perfect preschool.

The best advice I ever gave a friend was, "Remember, no one knows your child better than you. If you stick to your instincts and listen to your Mommy Voice, you'll always be doing what is best for your child." **M.B.**

Whether you are setting boundaries and limits at home or your child is learning them at school, it's beneficial to know how to provide the opportunity for your children to healthfully comply with behavioral expectations.

While it sounds basic, establishing clear limits on behavior is something parents get very little guidance about. Therefore, setting the limit on behaviors becomes an afterthought...and that too often leads to meltdowns and you the parent retreating into damage control mode.

I want you and your child to be successful in this. Let me show you how it works.

The Family Coach's *"Easy as 1-2-3"* Solution

When there is an unacceptable behavior that you know is outside the limit, you need to clearly set the limit for your child. Sometimes you'll be able to anticipate a rule violation before it happens, but sometimes you won't. There is no bad time to establish limits, but it's important that you do it as soon as you realize you need to, and that you do it clearly and calmly. Here's the 1-2-3 of it:

1. Identify and reinforce the family value at issue.
2. Name the rule or expected behavior.
3. Clearly communicate the limits on the behavior, showing the child what the successful accomplishment of the behavior looks like.

I want to help you become proactive with everyday problems. Below are several examples of common "off-limits" behaviors and how you can address them.

Behavior #1: Hitting

Step #1: Reinforce the Family Value.

"We are a family who uses our bodies kindly."

Step #2: Name the rule or expected behavior.

"We keep our hands to ourselves."

Step #3: Clearly communicate the limits on the behavior.

"When we are angry we can talk about it, get our anger out through movement, or walk away in order to calm down. Under no circumstances do we hit another person."

In this example, you have not only clarified what is expected, but you have provided other appropriate options to hitting, while at the same time clearly stating: "We do not hit." You clarified the expectation, set the limit and offered an alternative behavior. Yea! You did it!

Providing your children with alternative strategies leads to behavioral success for your little ones. Children hit, bite, scratch, and hurt others prior to 5 years of age because they have difficulty modulating their behaviors and making alternative choices.

> ☞ *TIP:* Sit down with your child and write out alternative strategies to hitting or biting. Then, tell the child if they make a *choice* to use the "hurting behavior" they will have a consequence. Make the consequence simple, logical and immediate: "Jessica, you chose to bite your brother instead of stepping back when you were angry as we agreed you would do. First, you must do something nice for your brother, and then you will sit in the thinking chair for three minutes to serve your consequence."

Make sure that the consequences are determined ahead of time, not on the spur of the moment, and make the consequences as simple and discrete as possible. After the child has served their sentence for "willful non-compliance," you can practice re-doing the behavior using a new strategy. Remember, teaching is your primary role as a parent.

Behavior #2: Getting up from the dinner table without permission

Step #1: Reinforce the Family Value.

"We are a family who respects authority."

Step #2: Name the rule or expected behavior.

"When we sit down for dinner, everyone remains at the table until they are excused by a parent."

Step #3: Clearly communicate the limits on the behavior.

"When we eat dinner, we do so as a family. We wait until everyone is done before we leave the table. If you need to get up from the table, you ask for permission."

In this example, you have established the family norm for dinner table behavior. You can clearly establish other limits as well, such as: "If we do not like something on our plate we do not comment on it, we simply choose not to eat it;" "At the dinner table we take turns talking so that everyone is heard," "We use our fork and knife for eating," "We keep our hands to ourselves," "We keep our elbows off the table," "We clear our dishes and take them to the sink," or "We thank the cook."

Now, of course, you do not say this all at once like a robot, you assert the expected behavior when there is cause for concern that a child might cross over the line of demarcation. You state the expectation to reinforce future behavioral choices.

Behavior #3: Teasing a peer at school

Step #1: Reinforce the Family Value.

"We are a family who speaks politely to and about others."

Step #2: Name the "rule" or expected behavior.

"We speak kindly about others."

Step #3: Clearly communicate the limits on the behavior.

"We do not participate in teasing. When someone is being teased, we tell a teacher or we walk away."

Teasing is a particularly common part of school life, but if you pro-actively tell your children you do not condone or support teasing and you expect the same of them, then there is no question when the circumstance arises.

There is no way that, as a parent, you can anticipate every possible rule, boundary or limit violation. Much of being a parent is responding to circumstances you never expected, like when your sixth-grader steals a bike or your third-grader participates in trashing the school bathroom. Communicating your values to your children is your foundation when unanticipated events occur.

Express dismay (Go ahead, it's OK)

Your family values cover almost all behaviors. If you are a family who "respects the rights of others," then stealing a bike is certainly outside that family norm. Since you established the values of your family clearly, and even in writing, it is easy to say, "I have trouble imagining how that happened, because we do not live like that."

As a general rule, the simplest way to respond to a limit violation or a rule infraction is to *express dismay*: "I noticed you hit your brother and I am not sure why you would do that when we are a family who respects each other with our bodies." This way explains the violation and also inspires contemplation of the action before moving to relationship-repair and Consequenceland, which we will discuss in Chapter 10.

Why do children test the limits?

Learning where the lines are drawn is a basic part of childhood. Children generally test the limits to make sure that they are firmly established and to determine whether they are really required to stay within them. Testing the limits is often done for several other reasons too:

1. To establish the hierarchy of power in the relationship.
2. To gain control of the situation.
3. To assert one's needs.
4. To try to move the limit or boundary.
5. To get what one wants.

Testing the limits is also a method of *defining one's identity*. If your 8-year-old knows she cannot wear makeup to school, she might come into the kitchen on a school day with makeup on, just to see what your reaction will be. Will you be calm and consistent and simply state that behavior is not allowed and politely request for her to remove the makeup so she can go to school? Or, will you be emotive, perhaps even angry, and provide a setting where an argument can begin?

When you think about defining one's identity through behavior, clothing choices, word choices and friendship choices, it is easy to see that upper and lower limits on acceptable choices will let your child know what they can and cannot do, who they can and cannot play with, where they can and cannot go, etc.

Limits help your children define what traits they wish to take on as their own, and which traits they will leave to others.

Some people test the limits through adulthood. Some people simply wonder, "How much can I get away with?" Clearly, there are inappropriate ways to test limits, but there are appropriate instances, as well.

Appropriate Limit-Testing

There are times when testing the limits is appropriate and even expected. While we have spoken a lot about skill deficits, we haven't yet explored the next steps in *skill development*. Skill development is surprisingly sequential. As an example, babies usually develop gross motor skills in a general order. In the first few months they push up and roll over, at 4 months they sit assisted, and around 6 months they sit unassisted and begin to crawl. As children develop skills it is normal, expected, and desirable for them to test the limits – it is how they grow.

Children will appropriately test the limits when they are on the brink of a new skill. As an example, when a child is beginning to walk, he will test his skills and yours as he ventures across the floor, first walking around holding on to the furniture and then roaming across the room with excitement and surprise.

Children will also appropriately test the limits when they are ready to move on to a new skill, but the opportunity for them to exhibit the skill is not being provided. The following example is about a toddler, but the moral of the story holds true for all ages... and all parents!

The Day Samson Fed Himself

One day, an 18-month-old boy named Samson was sitting in his high chair anxiously awaiting lunch. His mother sat down and started feeding him, but he reached out and threw the food on the floor. His mother reprimanded him, picked up the food, and, sure enough, Samson swiped the bowl onto the floor again. His mother looked at me, frustrated, and said, "See how he misbehaves?"

It struck me that this mom, loving as she was, was still feeding her 18-month-old herself. Normally, by 9 to 12 months, children are picking up finger foods by themselves. I started to play detective. I asked the mom, "Does Samson ever feed himself?" She responded, "Yes, but he makes a mess, so I do it." "What foods does he like to feed himself?" I asked. She replied, "Well, he likes to use the spoon, but he gets it on his face and the floor, so I won't let him touch the spoon."

Therein lay the challenge. Around 15 months, children begin using utensils to feed themselves. So I asked, "If Samson were sending you a message by throwing the food on the floor, what might it be?" Mom looked puzzled. I suggested an experiment. We laid out a few age-appropriate finger foods to see what he would do with them. Samson smiled and started picking up the food and putting it in his mouth. With that success under our belt, I suggested his mother give him the spoon. With remarkable dexterity Samson started spooning the peas off the plate and into his mouth.

It may have been true that at one time Samson had made a mess, but children's skills grow rapidly and now he was ready to feed himself. Happy mom, happy toddler. This is a great example of when children appropriately test limits or send a "message" to a parent. We need to play detective and ask, "What is the meaning of the behavior" in order to decide what strategies will be useful.

Why do children misbehave?

If you attend a workshop or parenting class, you are likely to hear that children misbehave for four common reasons: attention, power, revenge or inadequacy. Yet, when I ask parents the meanings behind behavior, they often come up with a broader range of reasons children misbehave.

Children may misbehave due to:

1. **Developmental delays:** Children who experience language, motor, social and cognitive delays may misbehave due to developmental challenges.

2. **Illness:** When we don't feel well, we often don't have the skills, patience, calming power or thinking ability to do the right thing. Neither does your child.

3. **Boredom:** This is common in school when topics and activities do not stimulate the brain enough to keep it engaged.

4. **Frustration and anger:** When tasks, people or experiences lead us to frustration or anger, we are unlikely to do the right thing or make a good choice.

5. **A need for attention:** Most people enjoy attention, but it is normal for children to seek an especially high level of the stimulation and comfort of attention, love and nurturance.

6. **Anxiety:** Anxiety is simply fear turned on its side. They both come from the same biological brain system, the limbic system. Many times, children misbehave because they are anxious, afraid or both, even if they don't have the language skills to communicate their concerns or fears. This could be anything from monsters under the bed to a teacher who intimidates them.

7. **Low self-esteem:** When children do not regard themselves very highly, part of them figures, "Who cares. Whatever. Things are no good for me now so why should I comply?" (Be aware that children can experience true depression, in which case you may wish to consult with a professional.)

8. **Misunderstanding:** Sometimes children misunderstand what is expected of them. This can be due to communication, listening or attention challenges.

9. **Pacing problems:** The internal motor of some children runs too high, making their internal pacing and speed difficult to manage themselves.

10. **Communication challenges:** Due to receptive and/or expressive language issues, some children do not have the foundational communication skills to exhibit appropriate behaviors.

11. **Sabotage:** While parents are generally well meaning, they can mis-communicate with their children, expect skills beyond the child's ability, or interfere with learning because of their own anger and skill deficits. (See "Unintentional Sabotage," on p. 115.)

12. **Sensory overload:** Some children experience overloads to their nervous system that lead to acting up and acting out. Sensory calming skills need to be employed.

One method for stepping back and collecting data before you form an opinion or intervene is to ask yourself: "What is the meaning of the behavior?" "What underlies this behavior?" "Why is it occurring?" and "What factors are reinforcing this behavior?" This is where your detective skills come in handy. When you do determine what's really going on with your child, then you are well positioned to take effective action. In fact, there are three steps to intervening: data collection, decision-making and intervention.

Why Sarah Wouldn't Stay in Bed
(and how we solved the mystery)

Here is a case for The Family Coach Detective. Six-year-old Sarah refuses to stay in her bed. Let's get sleuthing!

Before we identify the reason for her *misbehavior*, we need to wonder aloud:

+ What is Sarah gaining when she climbs out of bed?

+ What is reinforcing her getting out of bed?

+ Is there a message here?

The answers will not tell us the meaning of her misbehavior, but rather the meaning behind her *behavior*. Let's apply what we have learned and ask some more valuable questions:

+ Have Sarah's parents clearly stated their expectation that she is to remain in bed at bedtime?

+ Does Sarah have an evening routine that is consistent?

+ Have Sarah's parents used visual and auditory signals that tell Sarah's brain it is time for bed?

+ What about Sarah's environment tells her, "Get up, Sarah. It's not time to sleep?"

With a little inquiry we learn that:

1. Sarah routinely falls asleep at 3:15 pm on the ride home from preschool. She sleeps for 30-45 minutes and is hard to rouse from her catnap.

2. Sarah's parents say they have an evening routine, but they have never written it down as a family, and the components of the bedtime routine are rarely done in the same order. So, no true routine.

3. Sarah's older brother and sister loudly watch TV, play on the computer and talk to their friends on the telephone until 10:30 or 11:00 pm, while Sarah is expected to get in bed and go to sleep between 8:00 and 8:30 pm.

It takes just a few minutes of examination to note that:

1. Sarah is not tired at 8:00 pm. She has had a nap. While children's sleep habits vary, after 2 years of age, you can generally add 6 hours to the time they last woke up to determine the hour they are likely to be tired again. Sarah is a smart cookie. She takes a nap so that she can stay up until the teens in the family go to sleep. After all, 4 + 6 = 10...10:00 pm, that is.

2. Sarah's body is not getting used to a consistent routine because the family does not have one. If she were to eat, play with her family, bathe, brush her teeth, put on her pajamas, read goodnight stories, and then have lights out, her body would start to understand when sleep is arriving. This would allow her brain to begin its calming process, which easily takes an hour or so for most children. (See p. 166 for more about bedtime routines)

3. The environment is bright, noisy and stimulating. This tells her brain, "Hey there's still more fun to be had here. Stay up and join in!"

Isn't it amazing how just a little examination leads quickly to the solutions. You have already observed what needs to change. Before you read further, take out a piece of paper and generate solutions to this challenge. How would you fix this bedtime rebellion?

Now, compare your notes to some of the solutions we are generating together to solve this challenge:

1. Sarah is not physically ready to go to sleep at the designated time. It is clear that the afternoon rest is interrupting her ability to go to sleep on time. So we have a few choices. First, we can push back her bedtime and allow her to replenish her body and brain in the afternoon without negative consequences. If we push bedtime back 30-45 minutes, it is likely that Sarah will be more physically ready to sleep. If pushing back the sleep hour does not suit the needs of the family, we can work to keep Sarah engaged in the car ride so that she does not sleep. You can make her a portable art center and encourage her to do art on the way home or you can sing with her on the car ride home.

2. The family does not have a consistent bedtime routine. This family will be well served to establish a bedtime routine *in writing*. If the family encourages Sarah to write out the routine, she will be better equipped and motivated to follow the routine. If she prefers to draw her routine, that's fine too – it all helps with buy-in. At first, she may need help following the routine. Her parents will assist her with verbal cues and Sarah will be rewarded with family activities when she shows compliance with the routine.

3. The environmental cues tell Sarah's brain to stay up, not sleep. The environment needs to be conducive to sleeping. The lights in the house need to be dimmed and environmental cues such as soft music or a white noise machine can signal that it is time to sleep. The older children can also help Sarah, and not hinder her. They can watch TV, read, play music or play games quietly while Sarah goes to sleep. They can model "wind down" activities so that they are also ready to go to bed at the designated hour. Sarah's brother and sister can also read a book to Sarah or participate in a loving manner for fifteen minutes to help Sarah move to the next stage, sleep.

Your Piece in the Puzzle

There are times in your experience as a parent when stepping back and observing the challenge can be helpful. When we parents become too reactive and over-respond to our children's misbehavior we can quickly become a part of the problem rather than the solution.

How to Get Clarity

Take the time to examine your own behavior. What is your piece in the challenges your child or family might be facing? Think of a specific time when your family felt unmanageable. Write down the exact behaviors that were causing you discomfort. Now, use these reflective questions in order to examine your part. Is there anything you can change to help the situation go from turmoil to success?

- ✦ What was I doing?
- ✦ What was I thinking?
- ✦ What was I saying?
- ✦ Was I tired?
- ✦ Was I rushing my children?
- ✦ Was I impatient?
- ✦ Did I have too much on my plate?
- ✦ Was I having trouble managing my own anxiety/anger?
- ✦ Was I disengaged?
- ✦ Was I parenting from a distance – yelling at the children to get them to respond?
- ✦ Was I expecting my children to exhibit skills they did not possess?
- ✦ What was the environment like? (Too loud, too bright, too hot, too cold?)

- ✦ Was another person involved in the conflict (Were they helping or hurting?)
- ✦ What did I need that I was not getting?
- ✦ Was I inconsistent?
- ✦ Did I say yes one time and no another to the same behavior?
- ✦ Was I inflexible?
- ✦ Did I need a more creative solution?
- ✦ Was I maintaining my own personal boundaries?
- ✦ Was I teaching my child the needed skill?
- ✦ Did I need help learning a new skill myself?
- ✦ Am I doing all I can to maintain my own sense of internal balance?

When you take the time to look at your own behavior, you often see clues to what needs to change to lead to more success. Often, we need to alter our own behavior in order to facilitate successful behaviors in our children. *Change You, Change Your Child* again! We need to be invested in the process of change. Improving your family can indeed happen quickly, but it takes dedication, consistency and a willingness to examine our own role in the misbehavior.

The Importance of Practice (and that means everyone!)

Just because you became determined that you were going to begin designing your life rather than being run by it, doesn't insure that your family will change overnight. You are learning new skills, rhythms, and routines with your children. Sometimes, you are best served to practice the new skills with your children. Take the time to establish a limit with another family member and have your children observe, make decisions, problem solve and intervene with you.

If your child wants to eat a sugary snack before dinner and you encourage them to eat a piece of fruit instead to stave off their hunger, practice this with your spouse.

Ask your spouse to be the child. Who said you can't have some giggles now and then?

Parent 1: *"I want a cookie now!"*

Parent 2: *"We are having a delicious dinner in thirty minutes."*

Parent 1: *"But I am hungry now."*

Parent 2: *"You may have an orange or a banana now but cookies will wait until after dinner."*

Now, engage your children. They'll love solving the challenge with you. Say, "Mommy is going to make a poor choice. She is going to go to the pantry and take a cookie. We need to decide what to say and what to do to help her make a better choice."

Parent 1 walks to the pantry and gets a cookie. Parent 2 looks at one of the children and asks, "What do we say?"

Child 1: *"Mommy, Dad said we can't have cookies until after dinner."*

Child 2: *"Mommy, you better choose to put the cookie back. Dad said no."*

Parent 1: *"But I want a cookie right now."*

Child 1: *"Mommy, if you make a poor choice, Daddy might tell you there will be no cookies at all tonight."*

Parent 1: *"Will someone get me a banana?"*

Child 2: *"Mommy, you know how to put the cookie back and get a banana yourself."*

Parent 1: *"If I put the cookie back can I still have one after dinner?"*

Child 2: *"Yes, Mommy, but you need to make a better choice before it's too late."*

You can practice this example in many different ways. You can practice bedtime routines, completing your homework in a timely manner, sharing a toy with a sibling, etc. Be creative and encourage your spouse or a family friend to model with you. You will all practice and learn together. And don't forget to laugh.

Summary

Setting limits and boundaries is an important part of parenting. They help your children better understand and develop good behaviors. While some testing of limits is appropriate, limits are originally put in place to keep children safe. Be thoughtful and consistent when establishing and reinforcing the boundaries. Always remember that you are an important teacher of boundaries for your family. Being clear about the boundaries and limits will model good behaviors in your children's lives.

CHAPTER 7

UNDERSTANDING SKILL DEFICITS
(AND HOW THAT IS NOT THE SAME AS WILLFUL NON-COMPLIANCE)

Y ou direct your family, guide your children and mentor those you love. You model patience, problem solving and respect. You hug, hold and touch your children, communicating, "I adore you." But even "perfect" kids misbehave sometimes. It can be hard to identify when a child is being willfully non-compliant or simply does not yet have the skills to behave appropriately. This chapter is all about in-depth strategies for identifying skill deficits and tackling them effectively...before you move on to discipline.

Yes, but... *"My child is openly defiant. How can I tell if it's because he can't behave, or he won't behave?"*

When I talk with parents about struggles their children face, what often looks like "willful non-compliance" at first glance is actually a skill deficit. So, what is the difference?

Willful non-compliance is when a child has the requisite skills and ability to exhibit an expected behavior but **chooses** not to. Willful non-compliance is an act of defiance. It's a way of taking control. When you ask your son to pick up his dirty clothes and he just looks at you or walks away, that is likely willful non-compliance. Here are the questions to ask yourself if you suspect that your child is being willfully non-compliant:

✦ Have you clearly communicated the behavioral expectation?

✦ Does the child have the skill to exhibit the expected behavior?

✦ In this time and place, and under these circumstances, is he able to exhibit the behavior?

If you answer yes to all three questions, you are likely experiencing willful non-compliance. If no, he may have a skill deficit.

It is my view that consequences and discipline most aptly apply to times when your child exhibits willful non-compliance – *when your child knows the expectation, possesses the requisite skills needed to exhibit the expected behavior, and chooses not to.* We will discuss all this in depth in Chapter 10: Consequenceland.

Now, if you happen to have answered yes to the questions above, hang in here with me a little longer before you skip ahead. Determining the nuances of willful non-compliance and skill deficits is important and can be challenging, particularly when your children are younger. Yet, with practice you will become more and more adept at observing your child's behavior and understanding why she does what she does and what makes her do it. Then you can make a truly confident and informed decision about how best to handle it.

Tackling Skill Deficits

Tackling a skill deficit is all about teaching skills to manage task demands with talent and competence. It takes recognizing what task demands are needed and learning whether or not a child has the skill set to accomplish them. Tackling a skill deficit entails three steps on your part:

1. Collecting data regarding what the skill deficit is.

2. Making a decision regarding how to intervene regarding the skill deficit.

3. Implementing the intervention.

   ✦ If the skill deficit is a child's inability to use pragmatic language (language that is appropriate in everyday social interactions) to get his needs met, then speech-language therapy might be in order.

+ If the skill deficit is inattention, then behavioral strategies may be beneficial.

+ If the skill deficit is a child's difficulty regulating his moods, calming skills may be in order.

Earlier, we reviewed how to determine whether or not your child possesses the skill set to meet a specific behavioral expectation. As a parent you have likely seen that there is so much growing going on between ages 3 and 8; what your child was unable to do one day, he may be masterful at the next. So you must remain a keen observer of where your child is in this developmental skill spectrum.

Here's an example of a preschool child with a skill deficit:

Jason

Jason is 4. He has been asked to leave two preschools due to aggressive behavior. But what the school regards as willful aggression is actually a skill deficit around communication and language development. Not only does Jason have difficulty understanding 2-part commands, he does not yet have the simple vocabulary and grammar to get his needs met in the classroom. As a result, he acts like a younger child, with a younger child's skill level. In this case, the skill he has is something along the lines of "What I can't ask for, I will just take." He needs a better skill, more appropriate for his age. He needs to be taught how to express his desire for something appropriately, and how to engage himself another way if he doesn't get what he wants.

Now an older child with a skill deficit:

Robert

Eight-year-old Robert is watching television when his 6-year-old sister comes in and wants to change the channel. Robert calls his sister a bad name and hides the remote. Their mother comes in and says, "Robert it is now Cassie's turn to choose a program," to which Robert ups the ante and responds, "I hate you, Mom!" The mother is offended and begins to focus on Robert's mean words. She now wants to punish him for his words. But she's missing the point.

The Territorial Child

This incident requires skill building. Robert is not simply being willfully non-compliant; he is in possession of something he wants to keep as his own. He does not want to share because that would feel like a loss. We would all prefer our children just "man-up" and share the remote, but that's not the way life in a real family works. Children, like adults, are territorial, and most often they try to control, maintain and protect their territory. With repeated experiences of parents "coaching" them to higher levels of skill, children will get used to how it feels to share (not so bad) and their skill will only get stronger with each repetition. But it takes practice...lots of practice.

So what does Robert need to practice? He needs to find...

1. Appropriate words to express his displeasure.
2. The skill to contain his frustration.
3. The ability to allow his sister the space to get her needs met, and
4. The ability to find a replacement activity in order to calm himself down and keep his body and mind busy.

It sounds like a lot this way, but he *will* do it with patient coaching. At the end of the chapter (Activity #2) I illustrate one scenario that Robert's parents could use to help him make the shift into a higher level of skill – i.e., sharing when he doesn't want to.

Managing Transitions

Every day, children need to make transitions. They move from a zone of comfort to a new set of task demands – something a little less comfortable or perhaps less familiar. Typically, the transition is about territory – giving up their space or possession to move on to something else. But that transition can be hard, which can lead to poor behavior. In the case of Robert, he needs to move from what is calming and enjoyable to a new, less pleasing task. This involves disengaging from his territory (control of the remote) and moving to the next activity or "task" (waiting patiently while his sister watches her show), which means managing a whole new set of task demands. "Ugh," right? Makes me think of how hard it is to get out of bed some mornings. Who wants a new set of task demands?

One of your most important jobs is to teach your child new skills. In the case of helping your children give up their territory and move on to a new activity, there are some preventive strategies you can use to help your child give up what she likes and move on to a new task.

Equip your child with the words she may need to express simple needs and feelings and then practice them together. Write down how your child plans to handle difficult situations and be on hand to help her implement strategies as needed.

What we're talking about here is **collaboration**. You and your child are on the same team in life. This doesn't mean that everything is negotiable (it most definitely is not), but that you are seeking to meaningfully communicate your wishes to your child and give her the tools she needs to succeed.

In the strategies below, as well as the activities at the end of the chapter, you'll see that they are based in this idea of collaboration. I'm going to provide you with a few strategies that you can implement at home; but no matter what you do, it should work essentially like this:

First, talk it out (*before* the storm)

One of the most effective ways you can help build skills is by simply engaging your child in a discussion about what works and what doesn't in different situations. The key here is to initiate that discussion while your child is calm, **before the tantrum or storm erupts**. Parents often wish to talk with their children about conflicts or challenges during the conflict. That is about the worst time to talk with your child about his behavior. Kids can't problem-solve well when they are totally wound up, and parents get too frustrated. Always introduce new ideas when your child is calm and rested.

Then, create alternatives

When it is time for your child to exhibit a new skill set, provide her with alternative strategies or activities she can put into place in order to transition with comfort and ease.

Yes, but... *"My child has a will of steel and would never buy into something like this."*

I hear this a lot, and buy-in can be a challenge. But I have a wonderful tool in The Family Coach Toolbox that will ease your child's buy-in process and create the desired collaboration. It's the Green Light Detective Game – and it is one of my favorite skill-building strategies that I often use right away when I start working with a new family.

For Your Toolbox:
The Green Light Detective Game

This is presented to your children as a game that spotlights all the really good things they do, the green light behaviors that make your family a happy, peaceful place for everyone. Here are the basic concepts:

Green Light Behaviors

Green light behaviors are those pro-social behaviors that enhance relationships, keep children safe and foster development. There are thousands of green light behaviors – they occur in your home every day. To bring them front of mind, here are a few:

- ✦ took the trash out
- ✦ resisted hitting
- ✦ said thank you

- ✦ turned off the TV
- ✦ listened to music
- ✦ danced

- made the bed
- shared a toy
- kissed Mommy
- left for school on time
- completed homework

- was a good sport
- asked for help
- followed my morning routine
- completed my chores

Your role in this detective game is to identify and highlight those excellent behaviors – the "green light" behaviors – for your kids.

Yellow Light Behaviors

If there are green light behaviors, well then, there must be other types of behaviors too, right? Yellow light behaviors are warning signs; they signal that trouble may be coming. Often they will precede more serious rules violations, unsafe and disrespectful behaviors. Yellow lights differ from red lights in that they do not cause much emotional or physical harm. They signal that bad choices are being made and that harm might be on the horizon. Here are a few examples:

- soft swear words (idiot, stupid, butt-head)
- raising a hand to hit
- lightly pushing or shoving
- taking a toy from someone's hand
- not cleaning one's room
- leaving sports equipment out where it can be tripped on
- making an angry face as a precursor to aggression
- slamming a door
- breaking a safety rule

Red Light Behaviors

Red light behaviors are dangerous behaviors. Red lights are those behaviors that can harm the self or others emotionally or physically. Red lights need to be distinctly defined because they are subject to immediate and forceful action in Consequenceland. Few red lights should be occurring in a day or week in a healthy family. Some include:

+ running out into the street

+ letting go of a parent's hand in a crowded parking lot

+ hitting a sibling with an object

+ throwing a pencil at someone's eye

+ swinging a bat in close proximity to another person

+ hard swear words

+ talking to strangers on the Internet.

How to Play the Game (focusing on the positive and creating the buy-in)

In this activity, you will only need to focus on green light behaviors. Later on in the book we will discuss the other two. Now, I really want you to focus only on green light behaviors. Why? Because I estimate that in most families, 80% of the time we focus on negative behaviors, and only 20% of the time do we focus on positive behaviors. Especially when you're building skills, you want to shift the focus of your family to what is going *well*, not what is going poorly.

Here's how The Green Light Detective Game is going to work:

+ First, buy a large green poster board. Then, sit down with your children after school or after dinner and tell them you are so proud of all the great things they do with one another and around your home. Tell them you are going to play the Green Light Detective game and you want to know if they wish to play along.

+ Show them the green poster board and say that you are going to keep track of all the positive behaviors in your family for three whole days. Explain what constitutes a green light behavior, versus a yellow or red light behavior.

+ Write down an example of a green light behavior that has taken place recently in your home and talk about it ("Thanked James

for picking up her crayon when it fell off the table."). Hang
the green poster board prominently in your home with several
markers close by. Tell your children that any time they see
someone do a positive thing in your home they can write it up.
No need to write who exhibited the behavior – simply write
the behavior on the board. In a few days you will get at least a
hundred behaviors!

Be on the lookout!

Be a green light detective and stay mindful of any changes in
behavior you see in your children as they keep track of green light
behaviors:

+ Did someone check herself and choose to turn what could have
  been a yellow light behavior into a green light behavior?

+ Did any of your children start supporting one another in
  exhibiting more green lights?

+ How did you provide a supportive environment in which your
  children wanted to see more green light behaviors in your
  family?

+ Were the children able to see the positive or were they inclined
  to view the negative?

Spotlight green light behavior

Now, after you have played this game, you can place your children
"in the spotlight" for exceptional behaviors. After your list of behaviors is complete, tell your children that when they have shown excep-
tionally green behavior, you will give them a **Kid Buck**. Your child
can cash in his kid bucks for a special family activity, his favorite
meal or outing with Mom or Dad. (I like this tool too – you can be
the kid buck banker and decide how to use them in your family.)

What child doesn't like to be in the spotlight? Consider this: after
dinner one night, gather on the couch as a family and your children
can be "in the spotlight" for three to five minutes, one at a time.
They can do things like tell a story, dance, sing or show their artwork

with all the family members focusing their sole attention on the child in the spotlight. This, again, reinforces awareness of the behaviors we want more of in our family. Laugh, play, sing and experience the joy of green light moments with your family.

The whole point is to continue laying a foundation of skillful family behavior *before* we get to discipline and consequences.

🌿

Deputizing Kids
(another strategy that builds on the idea of collaboration)

When you tell a child directly, "You need to..." you'll often meet resistance. Resistance is a child's way of trying to maintain control over a situation. In order to move around the resistance and get your children engaged in the process of monitoring their behaviors, try deputizing them. Deputizing your children gives them further opportunities to develop positive behaviors while taking control of the situations for themselves. It also helps them observe the behaviors of others more objectively.

This strategy is often used in classrooms. You may have seen an elementary teacher give children different classroom roles. Typical roles include door holder, lunch carrier, front office runner and pencil clean-up person. Notice how well kids respond to being entrusted with a position of responsibility. These jobs are held in some honor, even.

You can do the same at home. Here's how: In the morning before you and your children head out to school, assign roles for the coming week, such as Wake-up Captain, Breakfast Captain, and Backpack Captain. Each of your children has a specific task to help get the family routine moving. In a large household, you can even put up a task board with the children's names and roles.

The Wake-up Captain makes sure everyone is up and out of bed at a specified time. The Wake-up Captain can do something like come up with a way to rouse the household, or call "Hey guys, it's morning! Time to get up and get ready." This role is helpful for getting the children on-task first thing in the morning so that they are ready to get dressed and get down to breakfast.

The Breakfast Captain is charged with making sure that breakfast is set out on the table and ready when everyone comes to eat. The Breakfast Captain may ring the breakfast bell to signal that morning routines are to be completed and the family needs to head to the table. Simple breakfasts like cereal and milk, toaster waffles or toaster pancakes are easy to place on plates with cups of juice. Some children really love this role. They may lay out new tablecloths and decorate the breakfast table the night before or place a surprise at each place setting. I have seen children set up an oatmeal bar with raisins, nuts and brown sugar in ramekins for a playful morning feast.

The role of the Backpack Captain is to make sure that all the backpacks are at the back door and ready to go. The Backpack Captain makes sure that homework, lunches and any signed permissions slips have been placed in the backpacks.

Deputizing your children with specific roles makes them feel like an important part of the family. Instead of having trouble getting through their morning routines, they are focused on their roles as Captains and enjoy the value of their different duties. Be creative. When the children have had enough of the specific roles, change it up a bit. You can have a Morning Exercise Captain, who leads the children through some jumping jacks and push-ups to get out their energy, or a Dog Walking captain who ensures that the pooch has gone out and done her morning business and sniffed around the neighborhood.

Deputizing your children also helps you so that you are not left doing all the chores for all the children. Please don't stress if breakfast is a little odd or the table set with the wrong dishes at first. It's not about doing it all efficiently, it's about giving your child opportunities to learn and grow. Remember, independence begins with taking responsibility for behaviors and exhibiting age-appropriate skills. Overall, children like to be masterful and independent. Get creative and watch the value of deputizing your children enhance your morning, afternoon and evening routines. This alone will improve the quality of your interactions.

These strategies are very simple, but if you use them regularly, they are very effective. If you are feeling extra motivated, I've included two more valuable hands-on activities at the end of the chapter. But right now, let's talk about the special challenges some children face.

❦

Seek to Understand Before You Intervene

As we've seen, basic skill deficits underlie most behavioral challenges. You and your child are on a journey together to learn new skills – your child is learning to function appropriately in the larger world, and you are learning to teach and nurture your child along the way. But what if nothing you do keeps little Emma from acting out at school, or stops little Ian's temper tantrums before bed? Understandably, the next step for many of us is discipline. But we still have a little more detective work to do before we go there; I'd like you to look for clues that there might be more to your child's misbehavior than first meets the eye.

Your child is unique, as you know quite well! He has his own temperament and sensitivities, tastes and habits, skills and aptitudes. He also has his own biological traits, strengths and weaknesses, some of which he inherited from you, some of which are environmentally based. On top of all that, he lives in a world that changes every day: marriages, divorce, parents with long work hours, parents at home, new teachers at school, etc. Each of these factors can profoundly affect whether your child is able to develop the skills you expect from him.

If you seek to understand what is underlying a specific behavior before you intervene, you can tailor your response highly effectively. In fact, it really is the only way to make interventions work.

Success Has Its Costs
(finding the time to stay mindful with your children)

Let's imagine a typical hard-working parent. Time and time again, I meet educated, professional parents who are being run ragged by their own success. They are so used to going at full speed every day that they no longer make the time to slow down and enjoy and their relationships. As a result, their children often appear non-compliant, spend too much time on the computer, misbehave at school, and are hungry for "stuff" to fill the emotional void they feel at home. Their parents aren't "bad parents," they're just caught up in the stress and demands of our modern world. And what they often see as misbehavior is more typically an underlying hunger for parents who are truly present in their children's lives.

When these parents pause to examine the quality of their relationships with their kids, they quickly understand that they need to be much more mindful and present with them. They see that by putting more emphasis on building secure and meaningful relationships with their children, they can once again nurture a sense of calm, joy and order in the home.

The benefit to your children of building mindful, secure relationships with them seems common sense enough, but there's also some interesting science behind it. Take a moment to learn the underpinnings of behavior, and you will see that more often than not behavior "problems" are in fact understandable – even biological and neurological – reactions to a confusing world. Once you get some of these concepts down, you'll be well equipped to identify what's *really* going on when Ian or Emma start acting up – and you can address it.

The Building Blocks of Behavior
(don't forget the DNA!)

Children's behavior is determined by three primary components: heredity, environment and the responses of people in your child's world. Let's start with the scientific stuff.

A Little Science, Please (not too much...just enough)

The human body is simply amazing. It is complicated yet simple, elegant and always changing. When we look at what makes up the human being, it all begins at the cellular level. Human beings are made up of cells. All cells in the human body, except red blood cells, contain chromosomes. In the center of each cell is an area called the nucleus. Human chromosomes are located in the nucleus of the cell.

In humans, each cell normally contains 23 pairs of chromosomes, for a total of 46. You inherit half of your chromosomes (one member of each pair) from your biological mother, and the other half (the matching member of each pair) from your biological father.

Chromosomes contain genes, which contain that all-important chemical: deoxyribonucleic acid, or DNA. Every factor in inheritance is due to a particular gene and its DNA. If you've got little ears, there's a gene whose job it was to make them. If you've got a heightened sense of taste, a gene took care of that too. There's even a system in the gene to tell it when and how to turn itself on – for example, when to start puberty.

We call the process of passing these genes and characteristics on to our kids *heredity*. Children inherit phenotypic traits such as eye color, hair color, height and weight from their parents. These are things that you can see with your eyes. But children also inherit temperament, cognitive styles, social interactive styles, shyness and other traits that are expressed through words, demeanor and behavior. All passed on through our chromosomes.

Let's think about how all this evolved. DNA contains the genetic instructions in the development, function and use of systems in all known living organisms. Think of DNA molecules as the blueprints or "recipes" that instruct any organism to make cells and proteins, and tell the organism what to do with this stuff. (Yes, we're organisms!) All growing things do it with DNA. We share about 98.4 % of our DNA with chimps. That's right, chimps. In fact, chimps are our closest non-human relations, closer to us than gorillas. What I find really interesting is that given all the complexity and beauty of this system, scientists tell us that much of our DNA has no known function. It's basically genetic gibberish!

How does this all add up for your kids? Your DNA, genes, chromosomes and proteins combine to make you a unique thinking, feeling and sensing individual. Because of your genetic constitution you move in certain ways, think in certain ways, feel in certain ways and sense in certain ways. Pretty amazing. Really, the core of you is your biology. The same is true of your children.

Biology, Medicine and Family Dynamics

When I am doing workshops I use three stories to illustrate the need to understand biology, medicine and family dynamics before choosing a style of intervention with your child. No one expects you to be a doctor. I am not a physician but I am a detective, a researcher and an active observer. Since knowledge is power, taking the time to recognize biological, environmental and social contributions to our children's behavior is beyond informative, it's fascinating.

Three case studies can help illustrate the importance of playing detective and honing your skills as an active observer:

Case #1: A skill deficit based in biology

One day I was interacting with a 3-year old girl during the course of a developmental evaluation. My role was to assess her language skills, social interaction, cognitive abilities and motor skills. She had been referred to me because she was having tantrums in school. This child had bright and loving parents who could not understand why she behaved so well at home but had been asked to leave two preschools. During the evaluation the girl did very well on standardized assessments: her language skills were above age level, her memory was excellent, she looked me in the eye, she showed exceptional attention skills and she was quite athletic.

But I noticed she occasionally turned her head and looked away when I spoke to her. When I would re-orient her by leaning over and looking into her eyes or gently touching her chin she would smile and nod. For a second, I wondered if she could hear me. Then I thought, of course she can, she's doing fine here in the testing environment. But I decided to test her limits, that is, look for the edge of her listening ability. So I stood up and told her I was going to get a glass of water and I asked if she wanted one. Before re-entering the room I knocked. I opened the door and noticed that she was not looking at me or the door as it opened. I got a bell from the instrument box and walked up behind her and rang it. She did not turn. I sang a few notes of a song and asked her to sing along but she did not.

It became clear to me that there was a problem going on but it had little to do with behavior and everything to do with biology. Before interpreting the test scores, I asked her parents to take her down to the Children's Hospital and have her hearing assessed. When the results came back she was almost totally deaf in one ear and had 50% hearing in the other ear. She was such a smart child she had been reading my lips! No wonder she struggled in the classroom. With the added noise, disruption from the other children and task demands that require being able to hear instructions, she was understandably frustrated – *really* frustrated.

Once she had a hearing aid placed, her behavior challenges disappeared. What if I had written a behavioral intervention plan for her tantrums, without knowing she was primarily deaf?

* * *

Case #2: A skill deficit based in medical illness

An even more startling example comes from a family I knew but did not see professionally. A child with autism went to the pediatrician for intervention when his Early Childhood Specialist noted that he would not eat, was losing weight, and was fighting back when he'd been put on a strict food regimen. The doctor noticed this boy was repeatedly tugging at his throat and he wondered, "Has anyone done a physical exam on this little boy?" An endoscopic evaluation of his throat showed that the boy suffered from esophageal ulcers. No wonder he didn't want to eat. But he didn't possess the language to say, "My throat hurts!"

Skill deficits and medical issues that affect behavior can also reside in the brain. Many of the children we see in our pediatric practice are diagnosed with Attention Deficit Hyperactivity Disorder. This is a brain uniqueness characterized by one or more of the following: inattention, hyperactivity and impulsivity. Other skill deficits I encounter in my practice include: Children who have trouble managing their moods, regulating their emotions, making and keeping friends, handwriting, turning in their homework, schoolwork organization, coping with anger, coping with anxiety, etc. The nice thing about what you have learned on our journey is that if your children exhibit these challenges you are now better equipped to help them.

* * *

Relational Factors

Sometimes, as parents, we are too busy at work, on our computers and on our phones to notice that we are ignoring our children. Read on and see if you notice any part of you in this story.

Case #3: A skill deficit based in the parent-child relationship

I was called by a school principal to assist with a 7-year-old boy who was misbehaving in the classroom. He would repeatedly disobey his teacher, choose not to follow the school rules, and got a lot of attention from the school administration because of his poor behavioral choices. The school took appropriate steps to assess the child's cognitive, social and academic strengths and challenges through psycho-educational testing. This boy was bright and had no underlying cognitive or learning challenges. However, his social skills were lacking and he missed social cues from his peers at school. He had difficulty responding to the cues of his teacher and would fail to alter his behavior, even in the face of pretty severe consequences, such as being kept in from the school playground or visiting the principal's office.

I attended an Individual Educational Plan meeting with school personnel and the child's father, for the purpose of coming up with steps to improve the boy's behavior at school. During the meeting, the father consistently made excuses for his son and did not appear to understand that he needed to be accountable for his behavior. The school personnel also got an insight into the father's own behavior when he took three phone calls during the meeting. He, too, was not reading the cues of the staff when they would look at him, clearly taken aback that he was yet again answering the phone during a school meeting. His behavior brought into question what he might be modeling for his son at home.

I wondered if this child was under-socialized due to the "benign neglect" of his parent. But he wasn't a "bad dad." He really wanted to do right by his son, but he too needed some skill building (don't we all). He agreed to bring the school's recommended strategies home so that the child would experience and learn about consistent behavioral expectations.

A few days later, I met the father and son at their home. As I chatted with the boy about his favorite activities, sporting events and his penchant for drawing, the father talked on the phone incessantly. Next, the child ran to his room to show me his toys, while Dad, with the phone attached to his ear, walked into his home office. I sat on the floor and played with the boy, who behaved quite appropriately one on one. He had a good grasp of language, shared well and was excited about an adult who was willing to sit with him and play.

When Dad came out about 25 minutes later I asked him if he could turn off his phone so we could work together. He commented that his clients called him at all times morning and night and he needed to be available in order to take their calls. It didn't take a psychologist to notice that the boy was getting very little mindful attention from his father. He was preoccupied with his work, mismanaging his work/life balance, and failing to interact with his son in a way that modeled relationships first, work second. He was a nice dad who just had his priorities out of whack.

As a starting point I wondered aloud what their family life would be like if Dad limited his work hours to the times when his son was at school or sleeping. We took the time to count all the hours he could work efficiently and productively when his son did not need him. The father was struck by how many work hours he would really have if he limited his work to times when his son did not need parenting. I left the home that day asking father and son to try a 72-hour experiment. I asked them to turn off all electronic devices during the son's waking hours over the 72-hour period. We made a list of family activities they could participate in together and I asked them to stick to that list for the 72 hours. Not easy for a busy professional, but he was willing to give it a try.

Dad called me the next day and said that he was amazed at what he had learned about his son in the first 24 hours. He said he loved to cook, help with chores, and be an active part of the home-life tasks now that the dad was off his phone. He said that he was becoming more efficient at his use of time and was surprised by how well his son was behaving at home. It was no surprise that this little boy's behavior at school immediately improved when he was "fed" with nurturance and meaningful time with his dad.

Our work, of course, was not complete, as we needed to make sure Dad could curb his habit of working all the time to the detriment of his son. But after a few weeks of planning, time-management and written strategies, this family was on a new trajectory to compliance, all through improvements in the parent-child relationship.

*   *   *

These cases illustrate the value of seeking to understand before you intervene. At first, behavioral interventions were employed before we had a clear understanding of what lay beneath the behavioral challenge. Not surprisingly, they didn't work very well. What you see in behavior is really the reflection of genetics, temperament and biology – along with what you add to the mix in your everyday words and actions. Knowledge is power, we often hear, and there is no one more knowing or powerful than you when it comes to building Your Extraordinary Family.

SUMMARY

Take the time to be a detective and analyze what may lie beneath a challenge for yourself, your child, your home or your family. Commit to trying to understand the meaning of behaviors and determining if your child has the skills to exhibit a desired behavior.

Consider the *who, what, when, where* and *how* of your family experiences in order to create and develop new ways of both understanding and shifting behaviors. Make use of these strategies and develop your own, keeping the core principles of understanding and skill building in the forefront. Go back and review your notes when new behaviors crop up. You are a skillful parent. You now have many tools at your fingertips.

HANDS-ON WITH THE FAMILY COACH

ACTIVITY #1

The Activity List Strategy

Achild's mind does not easily move from a place of comfort to a new task. Whenever a child's brain is occupied, she likes to continue that activity. Television is a great example of this. It keeps the mind busy with little or no effort (How many adults get sucked into a TV black hole against their better judgment?). Moving from that placid, familiar place in front of the tube to, say, getting ready to go visit Grandma is not neurologically easy. Tantrums and toe-dragging are a typical response.

Building blocks, cooking, coloring, playing sports and the like, take effort, even if they're fun. I've found a great way to overcome some of the natural resistance kids experience when moving from activity to activity: have a ready-to-activate list of fun things to do. This reduces the mental effort they have to expend to make a choice. Yes, believe it or not, to a kid, deciding to color takes mental effort. In our chaotic adult world, that can be hard to imagine!

How You Do It

First, tell your child that you're making an activities list for them so that they never have to be bored doing the same old thing. Invite them to help you make a list. This part, by itself, can be lots of fun. See how far their imaginations can go when they have a secure structure in which to roam – in this case, the pleasure of working on something positive with Mom, Dad, Step-Dad or Auntie. Try to come up with 30 activities, but feel free to add more. As always, I think inviting your children to color or decorate will really help everyone's buy-in – including yours.

Now you should have a nice, long, colorful list. Put it up somewhere like the kitchen, den or your child's bedroom door. Or put it in your Playbook. The next time your children are stuck, bored or arguing, you'll have a very handy tool to help them change their focus and move on to something constructive and fun.

Here's a sample list you can crib from, if you like:

Our Family Activities

Act out a play or story	Bake or cook	Bowling
Build a fort	Camping in the house	Carve soap
Charades	Chase rainbows	Computer games
Do a paid job (Ask Mom for a list)	Dress up and parade the neighborhood	Eat dinner under the table
Explore a museum	Finger paint	Go to an indoor play area
Go to the library	Have a circus	Have a fashion show
Have a talent show	Have a tea party	Indoor Olympics
Indoor picnic	Jacks	Join a book club
Make a coloring book	Make a home movie	Make origami
Make paper mache masks	Make play dough	Make up your own game
Make your bed inside out	Marco Polo	Movie mania
Play a board game	Play card games	Play dress-up
Play hide and go seek	Play I Spy	Play instruments
Put on a puppet theater	Put on magic show	Play kick-ball in the front hall
Play soccer	Play sports	Rainy day kit
Decorate my room	Scavenger hunt	Seed starting
Simon Says	Solve a puzzle	Tell old family stories
Throw a baseball	Tie-dye T-shirts	Train a pet to do something new
Treasure hunt	Walk in the rain	Water balloons

Be creative

I also like to use this list for other family functions. You can use your family activity list as a foundation for rewarding successful task completion. Instead of buying things for your child or promising a trip to an amusement park months from now (way too far away to encourage compliance), you can refer to your list of family activities for something to do this week, right now. With your list hanging in your family communications center or on your 'fridge, you can say, "Matilda, when you have eaten and cleared your plate, you and Mommy can create a puppet show."

You can also use this list to extend the dinner hour into a heart-warming and attachment-oriented evening of family activities. If you are overwhelmed, busy and tired, just play for 20 minutes using the list for ideas. Your child will get so much from just a little focused bonding time you, and even after a long day, 20 minutes is really doable.

ACTIVITY #2

❧

"The Walk and Talk Game"

One skill building activity I use with many families is a game called Walk and Talk. It provides a visual and interactive way for a child to process the fact that he won't always get exactly what he wants. It helps them to both moderate their own behavior and be mindful of the needs of others.

Set-up is easy. Lay out four 8" by 8" squares on the ground with masking tape. This can be done on a kitchen floor, on a driveway or even at the park. If you have square floor tiles in your kitchen or hallway they'll do the trick as well. During the game, your child will stand on each square in turn and answer a question for each one. The goal is to get to the fourth square. Do you know a kid who doesn't? I'll use an example to show you how it works. In this scenario, we will look again at Robert, who won't share the TV with his little sister.

How You Do It

First, I want you to determine what the desired behavior is. Here, it's that we want Robert to share the TV. So we start with square #1. This is where your child will stand while he tells you what he wants – even if it's not yet a reasonable demand!

> **Parent:** *"We are playing Walk and Talk. This will help you learn how to get what you want without breaking the family rules. This square is where you stand to tell me what you want. So, Robert, when your sister comes into the TV room and wants to change the channel what do you want?"*

Robert steps into square #1 and gives his reply:

> **Child:** *"I want her to go away."*
>
> **Parent:** *"What will it take for you to share the TV?"*
>
> **Child:** *"I don't want to share."*
>
> **Parent:** *"Sometimes you get to choose a program and other times Chelsea gets to choose. So what will it take for you to be able to choose a program and then let Chelsea choose one?"*
>
> **Child:** *"I want to watch my show first."*
>
> **Parent:** *"Excellent, you can move to square number two."*

Robert moves to square #2. The objective for square #2 is to get a commitment from your child to follow an action he decided on in square #1.

> **Parent:** *"What will it take for you to watch your show first then let Chelsea watch her show second?"*
>
> **Child:** *"Chelsea will leave me alone."*
>
> **Parent:** *"OK, so you want Chelsea to leave you alone while you watch your show."*
>
> **Child:** *"I hate Chelsea."*
>
> **Parent:** *"Robert, right now we are trying to get you what you want. Using mean words will not get you there. As a family, we use respectful words. So you will watch your show first – that is an option. What will you do when your show is over and it is time for Chelsea to choose her show?"*

Child: *"I'll throw the remote at her!"*

Parent: *"Using mean actions will not get you what you want. How can you get what you want, respectfully?"*

Child: *"Chelsea can watch 10 minutes, then I get the remote back."*

Parent: *"So if Chelsea watches 10 minutes, then that is fair for you, too. Do you just want to watch 10 minutes of your show?"*

Child: *"No!"*

Parent: *"So you get to watch a show, then Chelsea gets to watch a show."*

Child: *"OK."*

Parent: *"So we agree you get to see a show then Chelsea gets to see a show. Great job, you can move to square #3."*

On square #2, you have gently pointed out that what your child wanted was unreasonable. You have stayed calm and slowly helped him to understand the way sharing works and then commit to a certain behavior. Now Robert moves to square #3.

On square #3, you will talk about schedules and timing in order to secure the commitment. You will also generate a list of words and actions your child can use in order to cope with his disappointment and anger.

Parent: *"Robert, you are very close to getting what you want. Now let's think, what words can you say to Chelsea when it is her turn?"*

Child: *"Go away."*

Parent: *"If you say 'Go away' to Chelsea, you will not get what you want. If you say, 'Chelsea, can I have the remote after you watch your show,' you might be able to get what you want."*

Parent: *"Since you get one hour of TV a day, do you want to watch two half-hour shows or a one hour show?"*

Child: *"Supersonic is short, I want another one."*

Parent: *"OK, so at 3:00 o'clock when Supersonic is on, we agree you can watch that show. Then you will politely give the remote to your sister and she can watch Care Cubs."*

Child: *"I want another show."*

Parent: *"After Chelsea watches her show, you will each have one more short show you can watch. We will see those after dinner. What are you going to do while Chelsea is watching Care Cubs?"*

Child: *"Play on my computer."*

Parent: *"You get one hour of computer or TV time. If you use it up in the afternoon, there will be no time left for the evening. Let's make a list of all the other things you can do. You are so close to getting what you want."*

Child: *"I can go outside."*

Parent: *"Excellent. You can also build your robots, play at Daniel's house, walk the dog or make dinner with Mom. Let's get out the marker board and write down all the other things you can do. You can now move to square four."*

Robert moves to square #4. This is collaboration in action. You have directed your child toward making healthy choices using a 4-step process. He has generated solutions that you have shaped. You now have a time frame and a time limit. You have also helped him identify some replacement activities for when the comfort of the familiar territory (the TV remote in this scenario) has gone away.

Square #4 is the last step. This is where you child will go once he has figured out how to get his needs met. You close the collaborative decision making process by clarifying what your child has agreed to and what will happen if he does not fulfill that agreement. At this stage, you may want to bring in any other members of your household who are important to your child's new commitment (though only one of them will fit in the square!)

Parent: *"Robert and Chelsea, I hear you agreeing that Robert will get to watch his show from 3:00-3:30 and Chelsea will get to watch her show from 3:30-4:00. Can I see a nod of heads to* *show you agree? OK, what is Mom to do if I hear you fighting during this time?"*

Child: *"Send us to our rooms."*

Parent: *"Your room is a safe place where you can be happy. So we will not be going there for Consequenceland."*

Child: *"You can make us clean up the dog poop!"*

Parent: *"Let's just agree that if you fight, I will put the remote on the 'fridge and there will be no TV after dinner. Do we want to go into the TV room and practice sharing?"*

Child: *"No!"*

Parent: *"Then let's go shoot hoops. TV is not the only fun we can have here at home."*

As we saw in Chapter 3, children depend on rituals, the things that happen over and over again during their lives. These become special activities, often tied to a date, event or experience that you share with your children again and again. But in this case, the ritual is a simple learning activity. It's a bonding and growing moment for your child, regardless of the fact that it's corrective. These kinds of activities will effectively develop skills and foster that all-important buy-in.

CHAPTER 8

The Cave Man and The Thinker
(Understanding Your Child's Two-Part Brain)

✦

Children are a delicious mystery. Every child is born with his or her own style, temperament and skill sets. One of the puzzles of parenthood is to determine what kinds of parenting strategies fit the specific style and needs of each child. In this chapter we are going to talk about cognitive, sensory and social skill strategies for different styles of children. Let's begin with one of my favorites, The Caveman and The Thinker.

Our brain is the important driver in our behavior. Everyone's brain is different. Everyone perceives experiences differently and everyone develops skills differently (You might enjoy reading more about this in *The Executive Brain* by Elkhonon Goldberg, and *The Third Chimpanzee* by Jared Diamond). Through my interactions with the hundreds of 3- to 8-year olds who have been referred to me for in-home coaching, I have developed a paradigm of thinking that I feel helps both parents and children understand their children's sensory, cognitive and emotional experience. It all begins with the Caveman and the Thinker.

Inside Your Child's Brain

While brain physiology is complex and our understanding of it is evolving, it will be useful to you as a parent to know certain basics about that magnificent organ. In very simple terms, we have three parts to our brains: the neocortex, the limbic system and the

195

cerebellum. But two of those are most relevant to our (and our children's) thinking and feeling states: the neocortex and the limbic system. Let's explore these for a bit.

+ **The neocortex (The Thinker)** is located in the front of the head between your temples. It receives and stores information for decision making and remembering. It is involved in higher functions such as sensory perception, generation of motor commands, spatial reasoning, conscious thought, and in humans, language. The neocortex helps you parcel out actions and responses to your environment.

+ **The limbic system (The Caveman)** is a complex set of structures that lies on both sides and underneath the thalamus, just under the cerebrum. It includes the hypothalamus, the hippocampus, the amygdala and several other nearby areas. The limbic system controls all the automatic systems of the body and the emotions. Most importantly, it controls the survival responses – when scientists talk about the limbic responses, they'll use the terms **fight**, **flight** or **freeze**. The limbic system is particularly relevant when you have children with sensory overstimulation, mood modulation and anxiety issues. For these children, the limbic system is often on overdrive. That's why I will teach you some sensory calming interventions later, for your stressed-out kids.

The limbic system is embryologically older than other parts of the brain. In fact, it is called the old brain because it existed tens of millions of years ago, long before the brain developed higher reasoning function and symbolic language.

When you feel threatened, these protective responses tell you to defend yourself, run away or go numb. The limbic system doesn't have a memory like the neocortex. It doesn't know the difference between yesterday and 30 years ago. This is all very interesting and quite relevant to your parenting your child.

If you are going to employ strategies for cognitive and limbic calming, you need to get to know your child's Caveman and his Thinker.

Theoretically, our Caveman resides in the limbic system of our brains. The limbic system contains our automatic fight, flight or freeze mechanism that tells our bodies when stress is present. The brain is really quite interconnected; it's a challenge to say one domain is responsible for some behaviors while another set of neural connections is responsible for another set of behaviors, yet some research has been able to identify the primary sources of some of our behaviors, thoughts and experiences. Interestingly, the limbic system is also tightly connected to the prefrontal cortex. Some scientists contend that this connection is related to the pleasure obtained from solving problems. (If you enjoy a game of Sudoku or the crosswords, you know what this feels like.)

When we feel stressed and overwhelmed, our most typical response is to activate our Caveman. Caveman mode is generally quite visceral, often emotional, and sometimes aggressive. When children are faced with a task they cannot manage, they fly into Caveman mode and unleash anxiety and anger in a variety of forms:

✦ Biting

✦ Feeling immobilized

✦ Kicking

✦ Name calling

✦ Screaming

✦ Withdrawing

✦ Avoidance

✦ Stonewalling

The presence of the Caveman in our brains leads us to three common responses to perceived threat. When we experience anger, fear and anxiety, our most typical responses are to avoid, withdraw or fight back; i.e., fight, flight or freeze.

When you experience someone or something new, be it a person, an animal or a room of 100 people at a cocktail party, your limbic brain immediately tags these people and experiences as safe, vulnerable or dangerous, and then immediately goes into the corresponding survival mode. It all happens on a perceptual and feeling level, bypassing a reasoning process. I have an experience to illustrate this.

How I Met My Own Caveman
(and lived to tell about it)

In 1994, I was walking in the desert on a gravel path. It was mid-day and I was tooling along at my normal exercise walk speed, enjoying the beauty of the day. All of a sudden the hair on my arms stood on end. Frankly, I cannot ever recall experiencing this feeling and I was startled. My brain said, "Oh you're alarmed, your hair is standing on end." Then my eyes saw a mountain lion about 50 feet ahead of me. At first, my brain had difficulty comprehending what I was looking at. I saw a long tail – it was gorgeous, like an orange-brown swirl suspended alone in the air. Then my eyes saw two ears; they were slightly rounded at the top which confused my brain, as I am certain it was referencing previously stored images saying, *"no...not that... not that...no, not that either...."*

My brain was literally filing through pictures of animals I'd seen in the past and was trying to match the image up with a coyote, which I had seen many times before. But no, this was not a coyote. Before me stood a large cat-like animal, at what I perceived to be about waist height. My brain said, "Lynne, that is not a coyote. Walk backward, now!" So I did just that. As I backed away, I stared in amazement at this gorgeous creature and I realized that it was a mountain lion lying across in my path, sunning itself. It never even looked at me. It just stood there basking in the sun. At this point my autonomic nervous system kicked into high gear. My breathing accelerated, I could feel my heart pounding, I was awaiting a charge from this powerful animal, but it never came. I turned and walked quickly the other way. On that day, I was introduced to my limbic brain, for it assessed danger before my neocortex could even identify what was in my path.

Why It's Important to Understand the Caveman and the Thinker

Typical children – including children with the ADHD, anxiety, depression, OCD, and sensory processing problems – all share the phenomenon of "being human." The human condition is ripe with experiences that cause us stress, make us feel disorganized and drive our feelings of discomfort.

This is why I have become focused on children's skill sets, and not just their diagnosis. The diagnosis is only a *descriptor*, it is not who the child is. What matters when we are developing capable kids is what skills they possess, and what skills they need.

It is your Thinker, your neocortex, that helps you to manage the intense feelings and perceptual states experienced by your Caveman. Your Thinker plans, organizes, evaluates and executes decisions based on your feeling states. It was my Thinker that said, "Quietly walk way," after my Caveman sensed the mountain lion.

How can we calm the Caveman down?

Developing calming skills that help your Thinker calm your Caveman down is a large part of teaching yourself and your children self-modulation skills throughout life. There are many calming strategies your Thinker can employ to manage your Caveman.

If I Were In Your Home

After helping parents lay the foundation for their happy families, my next most frequent role as The Family Coach is designing *sensory calming* and *cognitive thinking* interventions for children. You know that my view is that the parents are the experts, so I teach these skills to parents who then implement them with their children. You likely already have some calming strategies you use with your children. Here are a few that I have developed over the years.

Sensory Calming Strategies

Strategy #1: How to Climb Down from Energy Mountain

Every person, whether a child or an adult, is well-served to develop calming strategies for moments of emotional discomfort, sensory over-stimulation and feeling management. As we have discussed throughout this book, many children exhibit skill deficits that underlie their behavioral challenges. It is valuable to understand the neurological components of these skill deficits and what to do to help your children and yourself be more skillful regarding the management of sensory stimulation, sensory input and feelings.

Sometimes children have feelings they experience intensely, but do not understand. You can help your child learn to modulate their feelings better if you take the step to help them identify how they feel, when and why.

One tool I use when I visit with a family is "Energy Mountain." Depending on your child's individual needs, this can be called "Anger Mountain," "Feeling Mountain," or "Anxiety Mountain" (which I'll show you, too).

Imagine that a child climbs an energy mountain throughout the day. Many children can walk down the mountain without letting their energy become uncontrolled. Some children hang at the top of Energy Mountain, feeling frazzled, silly, angry, agitated or anxious.

Draw It

Help your child "Climb down Energy Mountain" by drawing a large mountain on a large sheet of white paper or poster board. Talk with your child about activities we do at different stages of the mountain. Let your child draw activities on different levels of Energy Mountain. Use different colors to denote different levels of energy:

Calm = blue
Having fun = yellow
Getting excited = Orange
Over the top = Red

Have your child mark where he is on Energy Mountain several times a day, and you do it as well!

At the base we feel calm, we play quietly, we talk quietly and we are at peace. Up the mountain a bit we get excited, we play games, we play with friends, we play at the playground or at the swimming pool. Toward the top of Energy Mountain we are getting extremely silly, unresponsive, uncontrollable, angry or annoyed. Now it's time to "climb down Energy Mountain."

You know your child best. Write down calming strategies that you believe will help your child slow down and modulate his energy – like jumping on a trampoline, doing push-ups, breathing deeply, petting the dog, listening to music. When he is climbing up the mountain you can help him regulate his energy and emotions by offering him ways to "climb on down."

Strategy #2: Anger Mountain/Anxiety Mountain

When I am working with children on "Anger Mountain," on the left side of the mountain they write down experiences that make them feel calm (blue), frustrated (yellow), angry (orange) and furious (red). On the right side of the mountain they write down calming skills that could help them climb back down Anger Mountain before they explode.

With younger children, I tell them that their feelings are like a choo-choo train. Their train is happiest when it is "in the station." When their train is in the station, they feel calm, they enjoy playing, they have fun in family activities and they enjoy their friends. But, sometimes things happen that take our trains out of the station. A friend breaks our sand castle, or our mom says we have to put away our toys, or our sister calls our artwork "dumb." This makes our train rev up and zoom out of the station and up the mountain.

We need to make a list of calming thoughts, words and actions that can help us stay off Anger Mountain and keep our train in the station. Now, on the right side of Anger Mountain, your child can put pictures or words that would help her remain calm and cope with the situations constructively so that anger does not escalate and climb up Anger Mountain. It doesn't have to about trains in a station...it could be flowers in the garden, fishies in the ocean. Any metaphor that suits your family will do. What you are doing for your child is giving him the thoughts, words and actions he can't find on his own.

You can create an "Anxiety Mountain" project the same way.

What have you accomplished by these exercises?

Since you have now interacted with your children through their senses, the concept of Energy (Anger or Anxiety) Mountain is one they can use as needed. They have been made aware that they have tools they can use: they can write, draw and develop solutions instead of always calling to you to solve their challenges. This increases your child's feelings of mastery; they have words and actions "at the ready" to use when they are climbing up the mountain.

☛ **TIP:** Teach your children to think, not simply to obey.

More Calming Skills and Strategies

Children have a variety of temperaments, personalities, coping skills, and innate styles of taking action. Depending on their age, developmental skills and circumstances surrounding any given experience, their responses to hardship may range across the spectrum. When children evince difficulty coping with a life experience, their outward behavior may be a tantrum, tears or withdrawal. I meet many children with skill deficits who use avoidance and withdrawal to cope.

Curiously, whether children experience anxiety or anger, frustration or sadness, anxiety or worry, often an underlying theme is their own difficulty managing their moods. Feelings are part of the human experience, but being overwhelmed by those feelings can be distracting and disadvantageous in relationships. When children develop the skills to metabolize and manage their feelings, their daily experiences are generally more pleasing, calm and growth-oriented.

Everyday life is replete with ups and downs. In fact, we all experience a wide range of feelings and emotions from day to day and even in one day. The moments in our days fluctuate, as do our moods.

Giving Your Children the Tools to Manage Their Feelings

The children I meet who appear most resilient and skillful are those who best modulate their own moods. These kids do something called *metabolizing their feelings*. The girl who has the soccer ball grabbed out of her hands on the playground, then breathes deeply and runs to play tetherball instead of succumbing to a raging fit is happier, calmer, and more skillful than the girl who falls apart when that happens. The child who can identify, name, metabolize and manage her feelings is better able to navigate emotional obstacles skillfully. She is resilient.

If you don't already know expert mom Megan Calhoun, let me introduce you. Megan is CEO of *Twittermoms.com*, a wonderful online networking resource, not just for moms, but for all parents. Megan offers us an insightful calming tip she uses in her own family.

How I Calm My 4-year-old

I learned about this from my 4-year-old's yoga class. It's a great trick. Every time he gets upset, I tell him to do his "yoga breathing" – basically, this is just slow, deep inhales and exhales through the nose. It's amazing how well this works! It calms him down, gets him to stop and focus on breathing...and he either forgets what he was upset about in the first place, or

*he is calm enough to explain what the problem was. Now, he
even tells his younger sister to do yoga breathing when she gets
upset.* **M.C.**

As a point of observation, many of us are afraid to let our children
experience a broad range of feelings in life. We try to protect our children from sadness, anger or disappointment. These feelings are part
of the human experience. In a way, they propel and define our successes in life.

**I believe that parenting is not about protecting your children
from life experiences. Parenting is giving your children the words,
actions, thoughts and behaviors to metabolize their feelings.**

Metabolizing Feelings: Two Families' Experiences

Family A's Story

Recently, a mom and her two children were at a large department
store. The mom lost sight of her 3-year-old daughter and became
angry with her 6-year-old son for not keeping an eye on his sister. In
her anxiety and fear, she yelled at her son. Later, when the daughter
was located, she sat her son down and apologized. What she had
done was inappropriate. It was clearly her responsibility to watch
her 3-year-old, and not her son's. Further, yelling at her son and
claiming that he had any responsibility in the loss of his sister was
grossly mistaken. She acknowledged all this and sincerely apologized, but he did not want to talk about it. Instead, for several days,
he just huddled off in a corner of the family living room and cried
softly. His mom felt guilty and wished to repair his hurt. Without
the ability to talk with him directly, she needed to **work away from
the target** (addressing the problem indirectly) in order to help him
metabolize his feelings and repair himself.

Here, from start to finish, is how the situation arose and how it
was brought full circle to everyone's benefit:

Step #1: The mom had offered a sincere and direct apology for yelling at her son and blaming him for something that was neither his responsibility nor his fault.

Step #2: The mother had taken responsibility for her mistake by acknowledging that it was never her son's responsibility to watch his sister; it was the mom's responsibility.

Step #3: The mother had offered to make amends. She had stated that when you hurts someone's feelings, even accidentally, it is best to sincerely offer to do something nice, loving, compassionate, kind or useful for the other person.

Step #4: Since her son preferred not to talk directly about the incident, the mother invited him to spend a day with her doing something fun (an example of "working away from the target")

Step #5: He accepted the invitation and they spent the day at the water park enjoying one another's company. This provided them an opportunity to re-connect and for her to show him unconditional and fully-attentive caring for the entire day.

Family B's Story

In this family, the cherished pet died and one of the children was so upset she could not sleep. She cried much of the day and refused to hear a word about the beloved pet. This is another case where working away from the target helped this child metabolize her feelings and healthfully mourn the loss of her pet.

Step #1: Her dad spoke with her and acknowledged that she was very sad and preferred not to talk about it.

Step #2: He told her that he was also sad and that he was going to make a "calming basket" to keep next to his bed to help him with his sad feelings at night.

Step #3: He asked her if she would go around the house with him and choose things such as books, an iPod, earphones, art materials and a stuffed animal to put in his "calming basket" for if he got sad about the pet before he went to sleep.

Step #4: The child and her dad collected items, placed them in a basket at his bedside, and practiced choosing an item of comfort should he get sad.

Step #5: The dad then asked the child if she'd like a "calming basket" as well, and so they made one for her. Included in her calming basket were a few songs she and her dad created on GarageBand to help her fall asleep.

What is a resilient child?

According to Robert Brooks and Sam Goldstein, authors of *Raising Resilient Children*, resilient children have a unique mindset, one characterized by secure self-esteem, empathy and hopefulness. Similarly, Martin Seligman in *The Optimistic Child* writes about inherent styles of thinking and how you can help your child develop more resilient and optimistic thoughts. These books surely belong in your library, if not at your bedside.

Developing strategies to help your children calm themselves is an essential part of proactive parenting because your children may not have these skills ready at hand.

Let's delve deeper.

Art, Music, Movement and Dance as Skill Building Strategies

There are times when your child might be more willing to explore an experience in art, music or dance than they are in words. Using multi-sensory approaches such as these allows the child to explore an experience without needing to talk about it. Remember, there are many avenues to exploration with your children and not all of them have to include words. They can be about pictures, sound and movement.

* * *

Art

Imagine your child comes home with a bad grade on a test she studied well for. It feels bad to earn bad grades, especially if you studied extra diligently. You might tell your child, "I was just about to paint. Will you hang out with me while I paint something?" Then get out an inexpensive painting palate or piece of thick paper.

Place a few colors of tempera paint, some brushes, sponges and glitter on the table and begin with a large circle or a long squiggly line. If your child is interested you can tell her you are going to paint about your day. Ask her what colors you should use, what shapes you should use. Ask her to make a line, mark or squiggle and then turn it into something. Then ask her what it is and use the opportunity to explore her day in art rather than talking about it. Your child might even dip her hands in the paint and squish it all around the paper. The dark colors might mean something to her about her day. There are several art books you can get to encourage your exploration. You don't have to have a drop of "talent"... you are simply saying, I am here for you, I love you and we can sit in this experience together.

Author MaryAnn Kohl has written over 20 books on children and art. Her books are a wonderful resource for parents who wish to work with their children through art, not just through words. Her books will spark your creativity, encourage communication through expression and help your children to develop areas of their brain that will serve to enhance their life skills. *The Big Messy (But Easy to Clean Up) Art Book* is a terrific start for the parent who wishes to introduce art as a means of expression with your children.

* * *

Music

Imagine that your child comes home and is upset about a social interaction at school. You inquire and are met with, "I don't want to talk about it." You can respond, "We don't have to talk about it. I am going to play it on the piano." He is curious, "What?" "Well, when I was in school and I got teased one day it sounded like this." You play a deep chord on the piano. It doesn't matter at all that you don't know how to play the piano, just pound on it. (Or you can pound on a guitar or drum, if you've got one lying around.)

Choose a few deep notes and play a sequence of notes. "How did your day sound?" you ask. He might come over and play or he might stand and watch. He might even walk away. You can play a few notes and say, "Maybe it sounded like this." Play a few more notes or chords. If your child wishes to engage he might tell you, "No it sounded higher" or "There was more noise." Interact for as long as your child wishes, and play as he walks out of the room. Be compassionate and caring. Without many words you are saying, I hear you, I know you are upset, I love you and when you are ready, we can explore your experience.

* * *

Movement and Dance

Physical movement and dance are wonderful ways to help your children explore their feelings and experiences without directly talking about them. Turn up the music in your home and watch your children show you how they feel with their bodies. Have fun dancing like animals, being windmills and creating short skits or dances with movement and music.

Today's children often have to sit in school for long periods of time without very much physical movement. Moving your body fuels your brain. Consider adding "movement morsels" to your day with short bursts of activity such as jumping rope, jumping over small pillows, playing hula-hoop, running bases, biking, rollerskating or shooting hoops. Research shows that just 10 minutes of vigorous activity wakes the brain up and fuels the body.

꧁꧂

SUMMARY

As your children grow they will desire and need more independence, it is part of becoming an adult. Another part of maturing is responsibility. Responsibility can be taking care of the family cat, doing your homework on time, or being kind to other children; responsibility is taking ownership of one's behavioral choices. For much of this book, we talked about how you and your family can learn to demonstrate positive and expected behaviors until they become habits. Now, in this chapter, we have explored the realms of limbic development, thinking, art, music and movement, and how your child can develop the emotional and neurological skills to make better decisions about what they do and how they do it.

HANDS-ON WITH THE FAMILY COACH

ACTIVITY #1

Teaching Your Child a Song to
Help Remind Him to Stay Calm

Children love to sing as they learn. Consider adding a tune to this or make up your own song:

Volcano, volcano, I'm gonna pop my top!

Volcano volcano won't you help me stop?

Use my calming skills, help me take deep breaths.

Volcano, volcano I'm not gonna pop my top!

No one expects you to be Beethoven or the Beatles – just be yourself and have some fun communicating new ideas to your child.

ACTIVITY #2

❦

Teaching Your Child a Rhyme
to Help Him Stay Calm

Children find rhymes engaging. Here is one I use with children to keep the Thinker "front of mind." You can make up your own!

Your Thinker makes good choices,
Your Caveman pops his top!
You have to use your Thinker
To make your Caveman stop!

ACTIVITY #3

❦

Making a List of Calming Skills For Your Child

You already know how I love lists. Here's another. Take a sheet of paper and on the left side write out things that make your child "pop." On the right hand side write down words or actions your child can use to keep himself calm. Here are some examples:

What makes me POP	My Calming Skills
When my sister grabs my toys	*I can breathe and ask for them back*
When my mom says no	*I can go find something else to do*
When I get a bad grade	*I can study with my dad*
When I get in trouble	*I can go to my calming basket*

ACTIVITY #4

Suggestions that may make your Art, Music, Movement and Dance times more enjoyable

Art

Here are some supplies to have on hand:

acrylic paint	plastic plates
beads	rags
cereal boxes	ribbon
colored paper	scissors
cookie boxes	scraps of colorful clothing
cookie cutters	scraps of wallpaper
crayons	spatula
cups	stapler
foil	styrofoam
glue gun (for adult use)	tape
magazines	tempera paint
markers	tissue boxes
masking tape	tracing paper

oil crayons	water
old catalogues	white glue
old children's books	white paper
paint brushes	wood tongue depressors
paper plates	yarn
pencils	

You might keep these supplies in a multi-drawer mobile cabinet labeled and ready to go when your child is ready.

Music

You may broaden your "musical palate" with instruments you keep in your "music corner" in the event that your child wishes to explore their feelings, talents and experiences with music. Here are some instruments and equipment for you to keep in your music corner.

Accordion	Harmonica
Amplifier	Horn
Autoharp	Kleenex box and wooden spoons
Bells	Microphone
Castanets	Piano
Cowbell	Rattle
Cymbals	Recorder
Drum	Violin
Electric Guitar	Whistle
Electric keyboard	Wind instruments
Guitar	Xylophone

Movement and Dance

Consider these ways to get your family moving. I got this from SPARK PE, the nation's most popular physical education curriculum for K-6. You can order your own family exercise kit at *www.sparkpe.org*. Whatever you choose, the important thing is to move! It's good for your bodies, and a wonderful way to bond as a family.

Walking

Running

Sliding

Jumping

Hopping

Galloping

Tossing and Throwing

Rolling

Bouncing

Catching

Dancing

Climbing

Kicking

Skipping

CHAPTER 9

HONOR RELATIONSHIPS FIRST...
DISCIPLINE SECOND

༺༻

Through your reading, it is likely that you have arrived at a place where you now know that improving your child's behavior lies most in improving your relationship with your child. Together, we have explored how you can use *The Family Coach Method* to better define the kind of family you want to create. You are probably ready to take the steps to improve your relationships with your children or have already begun. If you are practicing mindful parenting by creating a values-based family you are already experiencing more peace, calm and joy in your own home.

You have invested a lot of time and effort so far in thinking about and planning for success in your relationships with your children. I am a parent, too, and I understand feeling tired, being overwhelmed on occasion and needing to breathe through the moment – so I know how big a deal that investment is.

Recently our girls were tired from a long weekend. We were all on edge and tensions rose. So, I suggested we lie on the trampoline and look at the stars before bedtime. This helped us shift out of a control struggle and back to sharing a loving moment with one another. We were taking good care of ourselves. While looking up at the sky, I thought of you, reading this book, and I wondered, how are you taking care of yourself?

* * *

Nurture Yourself, Nurture Your Relationships

As you begin to build stronger attachments with your children, think for a moment how you nurture them. I'm really asking you to ask yourself, *What is my nurturing style?* Based on our own historical relationships, we learn how to nurture ourselves and those around us in different ways. Nurturing your relationships begins with taking good care of yourself. So let me ask you some questions to get you started thinking about that:

✦ Do you take the time to care for your physical wellbeing? Research suggests that caring for your daily appearance first thing in the morning leads to a brighter day.

✦ Do you build quiet time for yourself in each day?

✦ Do you have your hobbies or interests close at hand?

✦ When you have down time, do you do what you like and enjoy, or do you spend most of your time each day completing menial tasks?

✦ Do you schedule your day? I mean, do you prioritize what you need to do and accomplish so that you have more free time for yourself and your family later in the day?

✦ Do you focus on the positive or do you go through the day noticing and even commenting on the negative?

✦ Do you assign specific tasks for specific days so that you know you will get them done without clouding your mind with worry?

✦ Do you take the time to compliment yourself and others on a job done well?

✦ Do you embrace your faults, accepting that they are a part of you, or do you place your energy in devaluing yourself and being unkind to yourself or others?

✦ When you are frustrated, anxious or angry, do you have methods for bringing calm to yourself, or do you "rain" on yourself or others with your feelings?

✦ Do you ask others for help when you need it?

✦ Do you have a written plan for yourself, your life and your goals so that you achieve small regular steps of success?

Pay attention to your feelings

You need to care for yourself in order to care for others. Recently a mom told me that she feels agitated and annoyed when not on her antidepressant medication. She felt ashamed that she suffered from depression, and said that when she starts feeling better on the medication, she sometimes stops taking it, which just makes her vulnerable to depression again. I thought she was brave to say this. She wasn't alone, but many people keep their pain to themselves. Just expressing her discomfort and embarrassment to a supportive person let her choose to get back on track.

As I tell my children, "We all have something we're struggling with. That is why some of it you can see and some of it you cannot; that is why we live non-judgmentally in our relationships." It can be difficult to accept that behavioral health issues affect us parents to, but they do, and seeking proper help, medical guidance and quality support is important to you and your family.

Take care...I mean it

According to NIH, approximately 26.2 % of Americans over 18 (about 1 in 4) suffer from a diagnosable mental illness in any given year.

While it is difficult to know exactly how many people experience depressive symptoms specifically (so many do not seek help), the estimates range from 17-20 million adults in the United States annually. If you feel you are experiencing depression, I hope that you will not wait a minute longer before reaching out for some manner of help, whether it's enrolling in a yoga class or consulting with a medical professional. I don't want you to put your mental and emotional health last in line on your family's to-do list!

Know yourself

You are human, even if you are a parent, with all the ups and downs that come with being real. It is valuable to know yourself, your style, your strengths and challenges as a parent – and this includes taking the time to know yourself better. Reflect for a moment:

+ Am I a morning or evening person?
+ What time of the day do I work best?
+ What time of the day am I most productive?
+ How do I best communicate with my spouse?
+ How do I best communicate with my children?
+ How do I respond to tactile sensations such as touch?
+ Am I huggy and feely?
+ What overstimulates me?
+ How do I best manage my frustration, anger and feelings?
+ Do I like to talk things out or think them over?
+ How do I prefer to communicate "to-do's"? Via phone, email or by making lists?
+ Do I tell my spouse and my children what I need from them directly or indirectly?
+ Do I delegate tasks?
+ Do I take on too many responsibilities?
+ Do I know when to say no?
+ Do I manage my daily responsibilities effectively?
+ Do I often feel overwhelmed?
+ Do I ask for help when I need it?
+ Do I make use of community support such as moms' groups, parent groups, school groups or religious groups?
+ Do I write down goals for self-improvement?
+ Do I schedule family meetings to manage our family well?

This is quite a list of questions, I know. You don't have to turn this into a test and there are no wrong answers. Simply reflect on yourself, your style and how you respond to your relationships and your environment. Reflection leads to improvements in your everyday life. So enjoy the questions, allow your thoughts to just flow. The answers you come up with may show you that there are areas in your life that are being neglected because you're so focused on helping others. This is normal for so many of us, but if you find that you are always last on your own list, your health, happiness and – most of all – your relationships will suffer.

If this sounds like you, I recommend a great book called *Take Care Tips*, by Jennifer Antkowiak. Written specifically for parents and other caregivers, it's filled with quick practical tips to guide your journey in self-care, from sleep advice to art projects to philosophy.

I just want to make sure that as you nurture your relationships at home, you always remember that nurturing your own wellbeing is an integral part of the process.

Now, let's shift our focus to the quality of your relationships in your home.

* * *

Honor Your Relationships

We all have priorities in our lives. Those priorities are signaled through our words, our behaviors and our interactions. Your priorities are signaled to your children and family in the degree to which you put your child's interests and needs first. If, when you get up in the morning, you go to your children's rooms and kiss them sweetly before you begin the rest of your day, you are communicating something to them about where they are in your daily priorities. If you pick your children up after school and talk with them about their day, take them to the park and play with them, you are telling them a lot about how much your relationship matters to you. If, when you get home from work, you run right to your office to complete the day's phone calls or check your email, you are again communicating your priorities to your children. What message do you want to give them?

What does it mean to honor a relationship?

In simple terms, honor is the degree of value, worth and importance you place on a relationship. It is granting another person a position of value in your life.

Reflect for a moment: How do you show others that you honor them?

+ Do I talk with my children eye to eye?
+ Do I share their exuberance when they show me their schoolwork?
+ Do I make their lunches based on what's quick or do I buy food that will keep them healthy, and that they in turn like?
+ Do I take phone calls in my car when I am with my children?
+ Do we make an effort to sit down to family breakfast and dinner?
+ Do I attend my children's sporting events and pay attention to them, or do I take calls on my cell phone while my children are doing their best on the playing field?
+ Do I involve my children in the tasks of everyday life such as cleaning, cooking and caring for our home? Or do I tell them "I'll do it" because that is easier than working through the process with them or dealing with pending messes?
+ Do I take the time to genuinely learn about my child's interests?
+ Do I schedule my work hours when the children are at school or do I work at home all hours of the night when they are home and need me?
+ Do I focus on what my children do right rather than what my children do wrong?

Take the time to answer these questions and write your own. What do you do to show your family members that they matter to you, thereby showing them honor and love?

No one is perfect, but when we strive to be mindful about how we honor our family, it builds trust, respect and love.

～

Introducing Attachment

In every family relationship there will be various kinds of "attachments," and it's important to be able to recognize them – your own and your child's – because they will give you clues to help you move forward in building healthy relationships.

As human beings, we each develop many "attachments" or enduring relationships over time. Of the many different relationships we form over the course of the life span, the relationship between parent and child is among the most important. The quality of the parent-child relationship is defined by many factors: temperament, character, environment, heredity, modeling and life experiences.

You may develop a different kind of relationship with each child in your family depending on their birth order, your state of mental and physical health, your age, the degree to which others support and nurture you as a parent, your financial security and the individual factors in your child.

From the perspective of The Family Coach Method, developing, honoring and nurturing your relationship with your child is central to developing a secure attachment in your parent-child relationship. Before you even have children, you are likely to parent as you were parented. With knowledge, reflection and experience you can alter your own style and behaviors. Remember, we accept and embrace our imperfections; there is always the chance to improve your relationships, past and present, so breathe through it and be easy on yourself.

What is Attachment?

Various authors define attachment in different ways. At its core though, attachment has to do with the ability to form and maintain healthy emotional and physical relationships with those whom you love.

There are also many styles of attachment, also defined in different ways. When we're talking about attachment between a child and parent or caregiver, there are generally four styles that social research has identified:

1. Secure

2. Avoidant

3. Ambivalent

4. Disorganized[1]

These categories can describe children's relationships with parents and childcare providers. The categories describe the ways that children act and the ways that adults act with the children that may or may not foster attachment.

Since this is a practical book, not a scientific one, we are going to review styles of attachment in a manner that applies to a family like yours. Let's examine your view of your own relationships and use the concept of "styles of attachment" to explore aspects of your relationship with your child or children that you like, and aspects that you would like to change. According to the scientific literature, the way a child is attached to her parent also affects how she will behave around others when her parent is not around. We will also consider how parents respond to their children and how this, in turn, impacts how their children see the world and then interact with other adults and, sometimes, other children.

We'll start with the first attachment category.

---

1 (Bowlby, 1969; Ainsworth, 1978; Main and Solomon 1986)

#1: Secure Relationships

This is the strongest and most ideal type of attachment. A child in this category feels he can depend on his parent or provider. He knows that person will be there when he needs support. He knows what to expect.

+ The secure child usually plays well with other children his age.

+ When a parent leaves a secure child in the care of others he may cry for a few minutes but will be flexible enough to seek others to calm and comfort him.

+ When parents pick secure children up after school or daycare, the child is excited to see the parent and eager to show the parent what he has made or done during his day.

+ The secure child shares his concerns with his parent. He sees his parent as an ally. He regards his parent as safe and comforting in tough times.

+ The secure child asks for help. The secure child may seek out his parent to help him solve an academic or social problem, knowing that he is safe in sharing and will be taken seriously.

What can I do to develop *secure attachment* relationships with my children?

1. Be consistent with your children.

2. Be attuned to their individual needs.

3. Respond to your children by getting off the couch, computer or phone and going to them. *Proximity matters* when you are communicating with your children.

4. Take your child's concerns seriously. This means acknowledging their feelings. Do not mock or tease your children. Sarcasm is painful and it cuts deeply.

5. Match your child's exuberance and excitement by sharing whole-heartedly in their joy.

6. Give your children your undivided attention in the moments they need you.

Parents who encourage secure attachments are attuned to their children's needs. They read their children's cues and respond to each child as a unique individual.

Over time, a securely attached child has learned that he can rely on special adults to be there for him. He knows that, if he needs something, someone will be there to help. A child who believes this can then learn other things. He will use special adults as a secure base. He will smile at the adult and come to her to get a hug. Then he will move out and explore his world, more equipped to handle frustrations or interruptions because he is secure in his relationships.

#2: Avoidant relationships

This category of attachment is not secure. Avoidant children have learned that depending on parents won't get them that secure feeling they want, so they learn to take care of themselves.

- ✦ Avoidant children may seem too independent.
- ✦ They do not often ask for help, but they get frustrated easily.
- ✦ They may have difficulty playing with other children their age.
- ✦ They may seem undersocialized, have difficulty reading social cues and appear to behave inappropriately for the social context they are in.
- ✦ Biting, hitting, pushing and screaming are common for many children, but avoidant children do those things *more* than other children.
- ✦ Avoidant children are calling out for closer relationships but they are not sure how to create them. Avoidant children are generally afraid of new and different situations, so being tender with them and inviting them gently into experiences is beneficial.
- ✦ Avoidant children usually do not build strong relationships with teachers and coaches. They do not regard adults as allies.
- ✦ They seem to try to care for themselves.

What can I do if my child seems to experience *avoidant attachment*?

1. Step back and observe how available you regularly are with your child.

2. Notice if you typically make your children wait in order to get their needs met. If your children feel you do not hear them and are unavailable this can make them feel afraid and insecure. (This is different from the appropriate type of waiting, such as waiting one's turn or not interrupting a conversation – respectful behaviors that everyone in the household exhibits.)

3. Ask people close to you (that you trust) whether they notice anything about your behavior that you might wish to change.

4. Turn off your electronic devices during family time, like dinner and trips to the park, as they are likely a barrier between you and your children.

5. Listen to yourself as you go about your day. Do you take responsibility for your behavior or are you often blaming others for what is not working? Working on this can help an avoidant child.

6. Take the time to actually sit with your children to do homework, play games or simply talk.

7. Observe signs of sadness, anxiety or being overwhelmed in yourself. If you find that you're struggling more often than not, perhaps it is time for professional assistance.

There are different reasons why parents might act this way. Some parents just don't know when their baby or child needs something. Other parents might think that it will make their child more independent if the parents do not give in to the child. Still other parents may be depressed, overwhelmed or fatigued. They find it hard to meet their children's needs when they themselves are barely hanging on.

Physicians and care providers who are working with an avoidant child may be able to help parents recognize and understand their children's needs. They may also serve as valuable referral sources for parents who need reinforcements such as in-home help, peer support, counseling or support from school personnel.

#3: Ambivalent relationships

Ambivalence (not being completely sure of something) is another way a child may be insecurely attached to his parents. Children who are ambivalent have learned that sometimes their needs are met, and sometimes they are not. They notice what behavior got their parents' attention in the past and use it over and over. They are always looking for that feeling of security that they sometimes get.

- ✦ Ambivalent children can be very clingy. Even as middle-schoolers and teens they are likely to attach themselves intensely to a peer for support.

- ✦ They often act younger than they really are and may seem over-emotional.

- ✦ Ambivalent children might tell you they are younger than they are, as they have not yet learned the skills needed to navigate the tasks of their own age.

- ✦ Ambivalent children often cry, get frustrated easily and love to be the center of attention. They are likely to misbehave to get attention.

- ✦ Ambivalent children may be used to inconsistent caring by their parents so they are not sure who to turn to in times of need.

- ✦ Ambivalent children seem to latch onto everyone for short periods of time.

- ✦ Ambivalent children may have difficulty self-soothing.

What can I do if my child seems to experience *ambivalent attachment?*

1. Work on becoming more consistent with your child.
2. Be clear with your child about their schedule and yours. When are you available to your child, what will you do when you are together?
3. Be on time. Ambivalent children do not trust people to do what they say.

4. Ambivalent children respond well to planning and preparation. They are more confident when they know what is next.

5. Help your child know that you are dependable and reliable. You want them to attach to you first, then to others. You are their primary attachment relationship. What they learn about relationships they learn from you.

6. Read your child's cues and talk with them about their wants and needs.

7. Help your child to observe their own behavior and the behavior of those around them. Notice the behavior, feelings and cues of children at the playground and on the sporting field. Your child will feel more confident understanding their social surroundings.

#4: Disorganized relationships

Disorganized children don't know what to expect from their parents. Children with relationships in the other categories have organized attachments. This means that they have all learned ways to get what they need, even if it is not the best way. This happens because a child learns to predict how his parent will react, whether it is positive or negative. They also learn that doing certain things will make their parents do certain things.

+ Disorganized children have not developed consistent patterns, rhythms and routines, so they may do things that seem to make no sense.

+ Some disorganized children have difficulty following classroom routines.

+ Some disorganized children have a hard time understanding the feelings of other children.

+ Some disorganized children may be scattered and inconsistent in play themes.

+ Disorganized children may not have early learning skills well established due to lack of exposure to education at home.

What can I do if my child appears to experience *disorganized attachment?*

1. Be more consistent in your verbal communication and physical interactions with your child.

2. Do as you say and say as you do.

3. Make sure to meet the basic needs of your child each and every day. They need to be clean, well fed and read to.

4. Get support within your community regarding health care, education, food and social needs.

5. Consider hiring a personal organizer or engage the skills of an organized friend in order to make your home a peaceful, organized living space. Chances are, if there is an organization problem in your home, your friends and network are aware and would appreciate the opportunity to help you out – even if it's hard at first to reach out and ask them.

6. Plan your time carefully so that your children's needs come first in your life.

7. Consider having a neuropsychological assessment or executive function assessment completed on your child by a licensed child neuropsychologist. There are many interventions now that can assist with helping the brain to develop more organization and planning skills.

One more thing: *attachment styles are not all or nothing.* Your child's attachment style is in part inborn and then developed through their relationship with you.

Consider for a moment what style or styles of parenting are dominant for you – we all tend one way or the other. Remember, this involves seeing how you interact with your children, your partner or spouse and the people around you. Really, it involves becoming aware of how you show your children that you put them first.

Create win-win relationships

Now that you have taken the time to think about your family relationships in a way that helps you honor them, you are on the road to creating win-win relationships. Being a stressed-out parent is no longer your style. You have shifted to being a more mindful parent, one who puts quality relationships above directing and bossing your children around. You have considered your children's strengths and challenges. You have considered what kind of communicator you are. You have established some goals for your home, your family and yourself. You are on your way to more passionate, fulfilling and joyful family relationships.

You are learning how to create win-win relationships for you and your children. Building skillful relationships is a win-win deal. Providing opportunities for success is win-win. Learning to listen and reflect is win-win. They are happier, and so are you.

THE "D" WORD

You or your partner may have wondered when I was going to stop talking about the "soft" stuff of parenting, and get down to the practical issue of **discipline**...the *ABC's*, the *how-to's*. While you may not realize it, all the way along we *have* been talking about discipline – family discipline, that is. Structure, clarity, expectations and outcomes. Once you decide to put The Family Coach Method to work for you, I am confident that you will wake up soon with a smile on your face, thinking, Yes, I really see what she was getting at. Building our family's home environment on a foundation of values, rules and skills while keeping our mind on the positive, not the negative, has led us to a calmer, happier place.

I truly hope that day comes, when there is less yelling in your home, your children are becoming more compliant, and you are getting to know them (and yourself) in a new and interesting way, where both of you are excited to see what comes next.

Yes, but... *"My child seems to thrive on chaos and tantrums, even with our best efforts."*

I hear you. It's not always going to be blue sky, I recognize this. Actually, I live it. And some kids are not going to buy into your best efforts, for all sorts of reasons. The moment you feel things are really not working, step back and watch. Stop intervening and observe. Your creative mind will help you find the answer.

Some of you will say, "Yes, I know. I do all this. I have a good relationship with my children, I give of myself in our relationship, I have stopped yelling and started breathing...and they *still do not do as I ask.* "

Then, what it comes down to is getting you back in the Alpha position in your family and letting your children know that *you* have the final say about their freedom. And if they want freedom they are going to have to live within your family Mission, Values and Rules. Bottom Line.

If your children still need more structure in order to help them become independent, skillful, compassionate and caring, it's time to move into a new territory where specific, carefully crafted compliance tools come into play:

Welcome to Consequenceland, the subject of our next chapter.

CHAPTER 10

CONSEQUENCELAND
(WHERE TO GO AFTER YOU'VE GONE EVERYWHERE ELSE)

❧

Whew! We've come a long way together since Chapter 1. You've learned about creating your family foundation and how to establish rules, boundaries and limits for your children. You have recognized that relationships are the primary source of constructive growth and development for your family. You've observed (and maybe already tried out) some of the many enrichment activities I've left for you. But there is probably one thing – a very *big* thing – you have been wondering all along. It's the elephant in the room: "What if I do all of this and my child is still willfully non-compliant? What am I supposed to do then?" A big thing indeed!

The reason I've waited until now to address this in full is that I wanted you to bring your family to a healthy, functioning state first. Any program of disciplinary intervention must be approached carefully and only after there is a consistent state of trust within the parent-child relationship. *Discipline is an art.* It should never be a reactive impulse. I have spoken about that before, but now I want to explain exactly what I mean...and give you the tools to work with.

Let me start with a confession: I really enjoy watching the nanny shows on TV. In fact, I watch them with my children. They are a source of conversation within our family. While we are watching, one thing my daughter points out is that the children are rarely given the opportunity to "repair" their behaviors or make a better choice before they are typically sent to time-out by their parents. (I'll bet the nannies *do* do this, but it just doesn't make very good TV.)

Repairing the behavior means taking the time to make a better choice. It's a simple action that we do all day long. You know how you want to say something that isn't very nice and then you catch yourself? In that moment you are repairing your behavior. You are making a better choice in service of a relationship. Repairing or choosing a new behavior, re-doing the action, ultimately repairs your relationship as well.

> ☛ *TIP:* As parents we all lose our patience once in a while. If you catch yourself and apologize for your mean tone, impulsivity or impatience, you are modeling "how to be" not "how not to be" for your kids. So forgive yourself for your misbehaviors, apologize and try to make a better choice next time. That's what you ask of your children; ask it of yourself as well. Believe me, they'll notice. And they'll learn from you.

I developed the concept of Consequenceland with the help of an energetic little boy. One day I was working with a particularly bright 5-year-old who had been running circles around both his parents and me. We were talking about how much he liked Disneyland and I spontaneously asked him if he had ever been to Consequenceland. I explained to him that it takes freedom to get to Disneyland, and that freedom was earned, not given. Consequenceland is a place where freedom is earned. That was the beginning of a strategy I've used and revised over and over again.

A Word About "Time-Out"

Up until now, you might have been using a strategy called *time-out*. Most parents in America use this discipline technique. The way I learned time-out in graduate school, it was a moment to take a breather, collect oneself and re-enter a social situation in a calmer mood, ready to comply with the social demands of the situation. Like many good concepts, in my opinion, time-out experienced "a regression to the mean," meaning that instead of remaining a higher-order parenting strategy designed to help "engage the Thinker" and "calm the Caveman," it became a form of punishment repeatedly misapplied by families, from mine to yours.

What's so bad about time-out?

Simply this: The way it is practiced today, children don't really learn from time-out. Time-out is often the last resort of angry and frustrated parents rather than one tool of many for skillful parents. Time-out is an appropriate place for children to go to calm down and reflect on the impact of their choices on themselves and others, but it is rarely a place of learning.

I don't really mind time-out. But I do observe that most parents have nothing more than time-out in their toolbox, making it rather ineffective. I am hoping to add some concepts that have more depth and meaning to the who, what, when, where and how of your behavior management techniques. Enter Consequenceland.

A Proactive Parenting Solution

In Consequenceland, children are provided the opportunity to implement behaviors that help themselves as well as the whole family. That's where the art of parenting comes in. You can learn it easily, with just a little patience and love.

The Family Coach Definition: **Consequenceland**

(n.) Consequenceland is a relationship-based proactive method for helping your children exhibit pro-social behaviors as they learn to live with the behavioral expectations of your healthy family.

After reading Chapters 1 through 9, you've likely realized that my view of parenting is 80% teaching and 20% discipline. I am convinced that the greatest part of parenting is teaching new skills that lead to wise decision-making. For that reason, when children break a rule or exhibit willful non-compliance, it is important to provide them an opportunity to make a better choice or repair the relationship they have harmed by their actions.

In the first 6 to 7 years of life, you are teaching your children skills to help them adapt, grow and learn. When shown how to manage their behavior, most children cooperate. But some don't. Lack of cooperation primarily lies in inadequately defined behavioral expectations, parents who focus on the negative, and children who do not possess the appropriate skills to manage their behavior in a pro-social manner.

The Family Coach Definition: **Pro-social Behaviors**

(n.) These are behaviors that center on caring, sharing and helping behaviors. Pro-social behaviors lend themselves to loving, not selfish, relationships.

With all your new strategies in place, you are learning that when you encourage positive behavior, remain calm, and are inspired to live in a happy and peaceful family, often just creating a positive environment leads to this reality. Many families tell me they never realized how much they focused on the negative, and that by making the decision to have a happy family (and it is often just that, a *decision*) and support individual growth, many misbehaviors disappeared.

Yet, for some children, given their temperament, their personality style and your family history, you may need to employ a limit-based parenting solution such as Consequenceland. You already know through experience that children need limits, and sometimes consequences, when they cross the line.

In Consequenceland we begin with opportunities to make better choices and make amends in our relationship...*before* we employ consequences.

Remember, Consequenceland is still a teaching tool. Even though the levels of response are designed to create some discomfort for the child, that discomfort is aimed at helping your children see the efficacy of adhering to your good wisdom and living with positive behavioral choices.

The Five Foundational Elements of Consequenceland

Behavior management in Consequenceland consists of five actions:

1. You focus on what you want your children to do, not what you don't want them to do.
2. You clearly communicate expected behaviors.
3. You provide the opportunity for successful behaviors to be exhibited.
4. When a rule violation occurs you provide an opportunity to make a better choice, offering opportunities to "repair" the relationship as appropriate.
5. You restrict your child's freedom to help your child comply with the behavioral expectations of your family.

While many parents focus on discipline, what really leads to the most success is planning ahead to prevent family conflicts.

Use your creativity, ingenuity and insight to create strategies that suit the specific needs of your child. In Consequenceland you remain proactive and focused on providing your child the opportunity to learn new skills and develop independence and mastery.

What Is Consequenceland? (a further definition)

Consequenceland is the "place" your children "go to" when they **choose** to exhibit willful-noncompliance. It is a pro-social parenting solution designed to provide the limits and structure necessary to help your children avoid willful non-compliance and to instead exhibit positive behaviors. Consequenceland provides proactive opportunities for children to make better choices.

There are three steps in Consequenceland:

1. **The opportunity to make a better choice:** Since teaching new skills is always the first line of response, we as parents want to provide an opportunity to make a better choice after a misbehavior. This is so our children's repertoire of good behaviors is broad.

2. **The opportunity to repair the relationship:** When a rule violation affects another person, the second line of response is to provide the child a chance to repair the relationship.

3. **Loss of freedom:** When a child is provided the opportunity to make a better choice or to repair the relationship, and chooses not to use these opportunities, then the child is provided a firm consequence that helps the child take responsibility for the choice. At this point the child chooses to give up his freedom. This is a progressive process that I will describe in more detail ahead.

As you can see, Consequenceland is responsive, not reactive. It must rest on a foundation of clearly established family values, behavioral expectations and family rules in order to work. Instead of allowing yourself to "climb into" (get sucked into) the conflict, you become the source of reason and calm prior to or at the onset of the conflict.

Collaboration is key. Parents and children collaborate on pre-determined consequences, thereby moving past control struggles and placing the responsibility for the behavioral outcome on the child who has chosen willful non-compliance.

Yes but... *"My child never obeys me no matter how tough I am. You don't know my child."*

Some doubting parents tell me, "OK, I'll try this, but we've done time-out and it doesn't work." Consequenceland is not time-out. Consequenceland is a method for requiring behavioral participation in established family norms. The result of willful non-compliance is loss of freedom. It is not punishment, but – just as it says – consequence. If you can remain calm, your child will understand the impact of loss of freedom soon enough.

Consequenceland has strong social components

In Consequenceland, the family works together like a herd, if you will, to manage the behaviors of its wild mustangs. Family members identify pro-social family behaviors in a calm setting before challenges arise. This increases buy-in of the children. Of course, we cannot imagine every infraction ahead of time, but when you have a proactive system based on responsiveness rather than reactivity, you remain a calm mentor, teacher and guide rather than an angry, out-of-control or simply frustrated disciplinarian.

Ready? Here we go, into the land of limits and the path to responsible freedom for your child. I'm betting that having this powerful tool in your toolbox will help you and your child achieve a higher level of cooperation, collaboration and contentment.

🐎

INTRODUCING YOUR FAMILY TO CONSEQUENCELAND

Introducing Consequenceland starts with a family planning session. For this meeting, you will need to make a few preparations.

We already talked about making a poster or marker board of green light behaviors in Chapter 7. So now, get two more boards for the yellow and red light behaviors. These will illustrate for your children their opportunities for making a better choice. Prepare to write down your ideas and post them in in a central place or your family communication center, if you've created one.

During this family planning session you will review appropriate responses to misbehavior with your children. Let them know that with cooperation comes freedom. When your children are responsible and accountable for their behavior – living by your rules, showing respect for themselves and others and doing "what is expected" – they are living in Freedomland.

The Family Coach Definition: **Freedomland**

(n.) Freedomland is the space in your family where happiness, joy and fun activities live.

Earlier, you may have made a list of green light behaviors that encourage your children's pro-social behaviors. Now is the time when you re-affirm with them that when they are living with these positive behaviors they are living in a happy place called Freedomland. Tell them that your goal is for them to experience Freedomland often, because this shows that they are living in accordance with family expectations and that they are positive, contributing members of the family team.

Explain to your children that when they misbehave, it is your expectation that they will correct their behavior and choose a better behavior so that they can remain in Freedomland. And when they misbehave, your family will have a strategy to correct those behaviors, and help them earn their freedom back. It's called Consequenceland. Collaborate with your children to determine how you and other family members will respond to misbehavior. Review the steps to Consequenceland and write down reasonable responses and actions as well as consequences – before they are needed.

Planning will include talking about typical family circumstances that lead to behavioral disruptions and problems in your family. You will discuss what leads up to the typical challenges and review with your children how peace, calm and learning take the place of furious outbursts. First, review the green light list and then go on to write out typical yellow light and red light behaviors. Write out alternative words and actions your children may use in order to prevent challenges. What you're doing here is *giving them the tools to use.*

Identifying green/yellow/red light behaviors creates a structured, visual method to help your children understand the results of their choices. As a family, you will have a vivid demonstration of the quality of your family relationships, and you'll see where work needs to be done ... or where praise is due. Of course, kids have a way of coming up with behaviors that you could never have anticipated, but your green/yellow/red light list will provide a good overall picture of how each member of your family is expected to behave. By doing this work with your family, you create a strong foundation for making better choices.

The Discussion

Here's what your family discussion might sound like:

> **Parent:** *"For several weeks we have been developing strategies to make our home life happy, healthy and fulfilling. We have enjoyed discussions about what kind of family we want to be and how we want to behave in order to have a happy and peaceful home. We have learned that there are times when each of us chooses to behave in a way that is not good for ourselves or our family. So now we are going to make plans for dealing with misbehavior. What do you think we should do when someone in the family knowingly breaks a family rule or behavioral expectation?"*

(Typical responses from your children might vary, but you have no worries, because you are Your Family Coach and will accomplish this task with a sense of calm and purpose.)

> **Child 1 (age 5):** *"You can send us to time-out."*
>
> **Child 2 (age 7):** *"You can take away my toys."*
>
> **Child 3 (age 13):** *"Nothing, our rules are stupid."*

(You can move past resistance by assigning children a role or task in the conversation.)

> **Parent:** *"Let's begin with a review of our green light behaviors. Jonathan, will you please go up to the green light board and tell us about some of the successful behaviors we have seen in the family in the past few weeks." ... "Please do not name the person, just describe the successes. Remember, we use our green light list when we are needing better choices but cannot think of one."*

Your list probably already has dozens of behaviors on it, maybe more, but if you haven't yet made a green light list, some examples would include:

+ brought dinner plate to the sink
+ followed the morning routine
+ read two books
+ said thank you
+ resisted hitting when angry

As we have learned earlier, our green light list becomes the list of alternate behavioral choices that members of the family made. When your child makes a poor choice, you can discuss, reflect on or even look at the green light list and choose a new behavior. Take a few minutes to review family successes, focusing on the fact that these behaviors are consistent with your values and mission. Bring the successful behaviors front of mind for your family. Draw a circle on a piece of paper and fill it with green light behaviors your children name and identify as positive choices for their behavior. You can let them know that this is living in Freedomland, where your children are able to move about as they wish, read, watch TV, visit friends and play, as long as they are living within the circle of your family values.

When I asked my friend Bobbie Sandoz Merrill, MSW, if she would like to contribute a favorite "How I Do It" tip for this book, she offered one that is similar to the idea of "living within the circle of your family values." For her, it becomes a "circle of choices," another way to emphasize positive behaviors. Here's how she explains it. (Bobbie, by the way, is the author of *Parachutes for Parents*.)

How I Help a Child Visualize Choices and Consequences

I have found during my 25 years of conducting parenting classes that the most clarifying tip I have is to draw a healthy-sized circle. Then put everything into the circle that is a CHOICE for your children – both the things they may do and the things they are required to do (including such things as friendliness). Everything they do that is outside the circle is a non-choice, a non-option for them, and must be clearly addressed the moment the child steps into that zone. **B.S.M.**

* * *

Now it's time to ask your children to define what a yellow light behavior might be. (If they name red lights, just jot them down and place them on the appropriate board for when you review red lights.) Make this an interactive, collaborative experience for your family. Respond to your children's input with agreement and, when necessary, rephrase their ideas for them.

> **Parent:** *"So I hear you saying that yellow lights are the warning signs that trouble is brewing. They are behaviors that are not green and might be leading to red. You're right!"*

Now, have a child write the list of yellow light behaviors. If your children are too young to write them up, they can dictate and you can write them for the family to see. Typical yellow lights might include:

+ Calling someone stupid, idiot, butt-face, etc.
+ Disobeying your parent when they respectfully ask you to do a task or chore.
+ Turning the TV on before all your morning tasks are accomplished.
+ Grabbing a toy from the hand of a family member.
+ Taking a possession out of a sibling's room without permission.

✦ Refusing to do homework at the expected time.

✦ Not telling the truth about a behavior.

Once you have a solid list of yellow light behaviors, move on to the red lights. Remember, *red lights signal safety violations*. Red lights are those behaviors that can harm oneself or another person emotionally or physically. Compliment your children on their participation and ask one of your children to write out the red lights.

> **Parent:** *"Akesha, will you please take a marker and write up the red lights we discussed and agreed upon."*

Have a collaborative conversation with your children. Use active listening skills such as **rewording** what they have said in order to clarify. Make sure that you agree on the red lights before they are written down.

Red light behaviors might include but are not limited to:

✦ Hitting, pushing or shoving

✦ Using hard swear words

✦ Driving or riding in the car without a seat belt

✦ Stealing something from a store

✦ Breaking a law

Once you have your lists of behaviors you are ready for a collaborative discussion of what should happen when the rules are broken. Below are two examples of a parent starting the conversation with a child:

> **Parent:** *"When we break a rule in our family, the first goal is to make a better choice. We do not live in a family that wants to punish each other all day long. We want to be mindful of the rules we break and we want to provide the opportunity to make a better choice. We want you to stay in Freedomland."*

Or...

Parent: *"In our family, we will work to provide one another an opportunity to make a better choice when someone breaks a rule. This opportunity is the first step in Consequenceland. It is the opportunity to continue being free and to live in Freedomland. You will have one brief opportunity to make a better choice. Making a better choice will often include an apology to the person you harmed in order to repair the relationship."*

Yes, but... *"My 4-year-old is not going to understand this."*

I am using complete sentences to describe the process so that you fully understand it. What you will say to your children will depend on their age.

✦ You might say to your 3-year-old, *"Jackson, in order to be free to play with toys, you need to follow the rules. Mommy is going to help you follow the family rules."*

✦ You might tell your 5-year-old, *"Emily, we have rules in our family. When you break a rule Daddy will help you make a better choice. Our green light list has lots of better choices."*

✦ You might tell your 8-year-old, *"Callie, you know how to follow the family rules. When you break a rule you will have one chance to make a better choice. I know you'll be able to do better."*

There might be some family discussion here, as this is an interactive experience, not simply a parent dictating new behaviors and children listening intently. You can agree with your children, incorporate their viewpoints into your statements, and thank them for their helpful ideas. Provide them the opportunity to delight in recognizing what allows them to live unrestricted as responsible children.

Here are examples of what your Yellow and Red Light posters may look like:

Yellow Lights

Behavior	New Words	New Behavior
Took sibling's belonging.	I am sorry I took your iPod, Joey. I will ask your permission next time.	Put the iPod back.
Got up from the table without asking permission.	I apologize for not asking permission. May I please get up to go let the dog out?	Wait for permission before leaving the table.
Refused to do homework.	I understand I need to do my homework now and I am sitting down to do it.	Begin homework.
Called someone a name.	I apologize for calling Jason a creep. I can say politely, "I am angry that you took my Webkin. Please give it to me."	
Used a verbal tone with an attitude.	I heard myself use a mean tone, I apologize.	Practice a sentence in a polite tone.
Rolled eyes at Dad	It was not polite to roll my eyes, I am sorry.	Smile at Dad to show you care.

Red Lights

Behavior	New Words	New Behavior
Aggressively pushed sibling.	I know to use my hands and body politely. I apologize.	Offer to do something nice for sibling like make her bed or play her favorite game.
Used hard swear words.	I know those words are not allowed in our family. I made a poor choice.	When I am angry I will take a deep breath or walk away.
Let go of Mom's hand in busy parking lot.	I should hold your hand because it is safe.	Hold Mom's hand.
Hit brother with a toy.	I am sorry. I will use my calming skills when I am angry.	Put the toy away for a week.
Went swimming without an adult supervising.	I know it is not safe to swim without an adult.	No swimming for a week.
Ran with scissors.	I know I cannot run with scissors, because I can get hurt.	Practice walking with scissors pointed downward.
Threw food across the table.	I am sorry. I know food is for eating.	Clean the dishes.

Now that you have developed clear guidelines for what behaviors fall into green, yellow, and red light categories, you have better communicated what types of behaviors are acceptable. You have developed a framework for giving your children the opportunity to choose an alternate behavior and you have introduced the need to repair relationships when you harm them. Let's take the time to look at little more closely at these opportunities.

Taking Responsibility

Talk with your children about what taking responsibility for their behavior means. It means they acknowledge they had a choice and they are accountable for their choice. No one else made them exhibit a behavior – they chose to use that word or action on their own. Remember the rule of respect? Taking responsibility often means showing respect – to your parents, your siblings, your teacher or the family cat. Help your child make this connection, so that they understand how their behaviors are part of a larger family ethos.

Avoid the Blame Game! Some families who have been more reactive than proactive engage in "the blame game." Your family members may be used to blaming other people for their own choices. It's an unconscious habit that is easy to get into. We all do it sometimes, but kids will learn to do it from us if we're not careful.

You might have heard these sentences before:

"You are making me mad."

"You made me hit you."

"You make me so crazy."

"If you didn't nag me, I would do my homework."

"If my teacher were not so mean, I would get better grades."

However, the reality is:

✦ No one makes you mad, you choose to be mad.

✦ No one makes you hit them, you choose to hit someone.

✦ If you are acting crazy, you are choosing to do so – no one is making you.

+ If your homework is not completed, it is because you chose not to do it.

+ Your grades are your responsibility – if you are earning poor grades, you need to take the steps to improve them.

For many families, taking personal responsibility for behavior is a new concept. Practice sentences that model taking responsibility for your behavior. Ask your children to name behaviors that they often blame on others and ask them to make a statement of responsibility. You can even talk in the extremes to lighten up the discussion a bit.

Exaggeration is a great way to get a child to look at a challenge from a new angle:

+ Slipping in the banana peel made me forget to do my homework.

+ Eating meatloaf for dinner made me get up from the table without being excused.

+ Watching TV late last night made me forget to put my homework at the back door.

Repairing Relationships

Another part of taking responsibility for one's behavior is repairing relationships that may have been harmed by behavioral choices. Families will always have conflict. Some degree of conflict is normal and expected. Conflicts help us to define our boundaries, clarify limits and even grow. But when we break rules that are designed to foster healthy family living and then harm others, we need to make amends for those behaviors and repair the relationship.

How I Do It
(What's better than being right?)

One of my favorite sayings I offer to our children when they argue about facts, possessions and experiences is: "You can be right or you can be in a relationship." In the moment they'd rather be right (don't we all!), but this reminds them that respect and kindness in our family is more important.

Take Felicia, for example. Felicia is a bright, energetic, strong-willed 8-year-old who consistently dominates her 4-year-old brother, Jason, hurting his spirit in the process. Felicia is a natural born leader. This is a strength when channeled into pro-social and cooperative behaviors, but Felicia has difficulty resisting the urge to dominate and control her brother. She wishes to direct almost every move he makes. When they play school, she is always the teacher and he the student. When Jason stands up for himself and says he wants to be the teacher Felicia calls him a "smart-tart" and tells him he needs to be the student. Felicia consistently breaks the family rule "We treat each other with respect" by ignoring her brother's needs. Felicia's mom and step-dad need to help Felicia contain her domineering style on a daily basis.

From the moment she wakes up and begins to "mark her territory" with statements like "that's my pen," "you aren't doing it right," and "I told you not to do that," her parents have to reassert their position as the ones in charge. It's not always easy, but persistence will pay off. First of all, they remind Felicia of her role in the family (she is valued but that comes with responsibility). Then they try to help her use her strength to develop positive skills (making her in charge of age-appropriate tasks helps and gives her a sense of accomplishment). They remind her what she may control (her choices) and what she may not control (other people) and provide her the opportunity to repair her relationship with her brother by:

+ Inviting him to be the leader sometimes.
+ Doing something nice for him like taking out his favorite trains and offering to play with him.
+ Engaging in a game he enjoys such as shooting mini basketball hoops.
+ Using active listening skills with her brother and reflecting back his own expressed needs and interests.
+ Giving him some space to be himself.

Learning how to repair the relationship is an important skill at home and at school. Young children easily feel "wronged" because they tend to be more concrete thinkers – more black and white

– than older children who are comfortable with abstract ideas and gray areas. So, reviewing with your children what they may say or do to harm relationships and then asking them what they could do to repair the relationship can be a valuable and even fun exercise.

Spare the Rod?

When you think of the word *discipline* do you think about punishment? Many Americans do. See if this feels more authentic to your family: Discipline is restraint; it is breathing through actions in order to make the best choice. Discipline is about learning to comply with appropriate social expectations. In today's world, it's easy to miss one aspect of discipline in particular, the importance of protecting, nourishing and repairing our relationships when we harm another person. That harm does not have to be severe – it can be something little like grabbing a toy from a child's hand or using sarcasm in a moment of inattention. We have opportunities every day to revise (re-do) our words, thoughts, actions and behaviors. I think this is true discipline. We need to have the discipline to take action and show we care about our relationships.

When You are the One Who Slips Up

There are times when parents make poor choices as well. If, as a parent, you are in a grumpy mood and take it out on your children, you can accept responsibility for your behavior, apologize and repair the relationship with a one-on-one activity. When you use a mean tone or forget your manners, repeat what you did with a better word choice or tone of voice so that you model positive change for your children. You may say to your child, "Let's have a do-over," as you correct your own behavior. That means you said or did something that you didn't mean, or used a tone of voice that was not loving, and now you would like to try again. Some parents think this is showing weakness, but it's not. You are showing that you walk your talk, can be counted on to take responsibility for your actions, and expect your children to do the same.

❧

IMPLEMENTING LOSS OF FREEDOM

As I mentioned at the beginning of this chapter, there are three steps in Consequenceland: **the opportunity to make a better choice, the opportunity to repair the relationship,** and when a child has chosen not to make a better choice or repair the relationship, **loss of freedom.** There will be times when you have given your child reasonable opportunities to make a better choice and/or to repair the relationship and she chooses to break the rule and not make a better choice. Hopefully, at this point you have made your green/yellow/red light charts and everyone is on the same page – your children know what is expected and have the skills to comply.

It is most important to implement loss of freedom only *after* your child has chosen not to make a better choice.

Assuming that your child has the skills to exhibit the expected behavior and is choosing to be willfully non-compliant, then consequences are needed. Consequences tell a child, "you broke the rule, I gave you an opportunity to make a better choice and you are CHOOSING to remain non-compliant." In that circumstance your child moves from an opportunity for change to a loss of freedom.

Freedom for a child is a space to play. It is also the space in which they relate to you as a parent or guardian, a nurturing person who loves them. A pro-social and value-centered method of teaching behavioral compliance to young children is to manage their freedom. Sometimes, restricting that freedom is appropriate.

The purpose of restricting a child's freedom is threefold:

✦ It gives children the opportunity to learn that with freedom comes responsibility.

✦ It allows parents to establish themselves as the people at the top of the family hierarchy. In a house where parents are not at the top, chaos and disruption become the norm. If parents remain calm, and avoid escalating a crisis, they reinforce their own authority and teach children where the limits are.

✦ It ensures their safety.

In Consequenceland, it is most important to make a collaborative decision with your children about what the loss of freedom will be *before* the rule violation.

Collaborating with your children helps their buy-in to the process. We have reviewed the importance of buy-in in earlier chapters. A good way to initiate the conversation is to sit down with your children and talk about the times when family members have knowingly broken a family rule and chosen not to make a better choice. Ask them to think about specific examples and review how it was clear that a family member had an opportunity to make a better choice but refused to do so.

Turn the attention to your Family Mission, Values and Rules and come to a decision regarding what will happen in your family when a family member exhibits a rule violation and willful non-compliance. These will vary from family to family; the important thing is that you write them down, commit to them and do not change them in the moment of turmoil. Inconsistency undermines the effectiveness of Consequenceland, and leads to escalation and loss of control.

As I said, loss of freedom is a consequence, not a punishment. This is a subtle but important distinction. In the examples and explanations that follow, I will use three consequences that I have found to be very effective.

✦ *Loss of an object, activity or person immediately following the misbehavior.* An example of this is when a child hits another child with a toy sword. The consequence is that the sword is removed to the top of the fridge for the day. Another example is when a child intentionally interferes with the fun of another family member or friend, the child is immediately removed from playing with that person. This method is most commonly employed in school settings and is quite effective for relatively minor misbehaviors. **I'll call this a *Level I* consequence for easy reference.**

✦ *The Thinking Chair.* Removal of the child from the setting where willful non-compliance occurred to a chair placed in an open space in the home. The thinking chair can be in the kitchen, living room or hall. For younger children the chair can face forward, for older children the chair can face the wall. This restricts the child's ability to see and participate in family activities. The thinking chair should be used for more serious misbehaviors. **This would be a *Level II* consequence.**

✦ *The Quiet Room.* This is a safe, enclosed setting where the door can stay open when the child remains in the room and the door can be closed and even locked if the child asserts his or her power and tries to leave the room. The quiet room should be used only very infrequently for serious misbehaviors or when a child has refused to comply with the thinking chair consequence. **This would be a *Level III* consequence.**

When things get tough and the mustangs start running, *it is critical to have your list of pre-determined Level II and Level III consequences written down.* We have ours on the inside of our pantry door. Over the years, our children have written about 5 consequences for *Level II* and *Level III*, but most often we rely on the thinking chair and, if need be, the quiet room, keeping it simple and concrete. When things get out of control, I want (as do they) swift, reliable, pre-determined options. They know what's coming, there is little argument, perhaps some tears and some anger, but the consequences are clear.

Of course, your consequences will have to be age-appropriate. You cannot send a 3-year-old to time-out for thirty minutes; they will not be able to comply. But you can identify a chair as the "thinking chair" and place it in a corner in your dining room or family room. If a child is willfully non-compliant, they have made that choice. So, they will *choose* to go to the thinking chair, away from family activities.

* * *

Now, let's look at some typical Consequenceland scenarios and see how it all comes together.

Jessica Makes a Better Choice

Jessica, age 7, and her sister Sarah, age 3, are dancing to music. Jessica is in the habit of changing the song to one that she likes better whenever she wants. Sarah feels left out and hurt that she doesn't get to play her songs too.

Before you go to Consequenceland, make sure that your child understands the behavioral expectation.

> **Parent:** *"Jessica, what is our family rule about respecting one another's needs?"*
>
> **Jessica:** *"But, Mom, that's a dumb song!"*

Now, move to the first step of Consequenceland: Offer an opportunity to make a better choice.

> **Parent:** *"Jessica, you have an opportunity to make a better choice. In our family we share. You can allow your sister to listen to her song and take turns or you can choose to lose your freedom."*
>
> **Jessica:** *"Fine. Sarah, listen to your song."*
>
> **Parent:** *"That was a good choice."*

OK, so what has just happened? The parent has asserted the family behavioral norms. She has given her daughter a chance to correct her behavior and Jessica made a better choice. Her tone was not what a mom would like to hear, but it was not over the top, so Mom now disengages and leaves the children to play. More often than not, that will be the end of it.

However, if Jessica continues interfering with her sister's ability to get her needs met, Mom might intervene with a distraction or replacement. She might need to come into the room again and suggest that Jessica play with something else so that the girls can each have their own space. Often, the very act of suggesting separation will enlist compliance. As I said, Consequenceland is not a tool that parents should use every time they meet resistance at home. There are so many effective tools: modeling new behaviors, suggesting alternatives, simply separating squabbling siblings. For a 7-year-old like Jessica, bringing other fun activities front of mind can be a healthy transition.

Naomi Chooses the Thinking Chair

Naomi, age 8, goes into her dad's room and takes his iPod without asking.

Before you go to Consequenceland, make sure that your child understands the behavioral expectation.

> **Parent:** *"Naomi, what is our family rule about respecting one another's property?"*
>
> **Naomi:** *"But, Dad, you told me to bring an activity in the car and I didn't have one."*
>
> **Parent:** *"I am pleased to help you find an activity. I may even loan you my iPod, but you cannot take my property without asking."*

Now, move to the first step of Consequenceland: Offer an opportunity to make a better choice.

> **Parent:** *"You have an opportunity to make a better choice. What could that be?"*
>
> **Naomi:** *"Dad, I already took the iPod. What are you talking about?"*

If necessary, move to the second step of Consequenceland: Repair the relationship.

> **Parent:** *"You know that you are not to take my belongings without permission. You can put the iPod away and make it up to me."*
>
> **Naomi:** *"I have no idea how."*
>
> **Parent:** *"Naomi, you know how to put the iPod back. When you do that now, you may then choose to do something nice for me, in order to apologize and repair our relationship."*
>
> **Naomi:** *"Dad, you are so mean."*

Note how Naomi's dad stays focused on the behavior, not Naomi's words. Naomi's words are a red herring; they are her attempt to get control. If Naomi is moving toward doing as told, she is moving in the right direction and Dad remains calm.

Naomi walks to Dad's room and returns the iPod to its home. Dad ignores the "you are mean" comment since Naomi is now complying. When Naomi returns, Dad can help her discover a way to repair the relationship, or, if Naomi still has an attitude and remains obstinate, Dad can remind Naomi that she knows what she is doing and her opportunity is passing by quickly. Naomi knows many nice things to do for Dad, but Dad can have a list of ways to repair the relationship hanging on the fridge (and bonus points for Dad if so).

If the child does not accept the opportunity to make a better choice and repair the relationship, then it is time to move to the third step of Consequenceland: Loss of freedom. Consistently and calmly invite the child to observe the appropriate consequence. In this case, taking something without asking might be a Level II consequence – the thinking chair.

> **Parent:** *"Naomi, you chose not to use your opportunity so you have chosen to lose your freedom. You will now sit in the thinking chair for five minutes."*

Dad sets the timer and Naomi is required to remain in the thinking chair. Naomi can hear the timer and knows that if she does not do as expected, more time will be added. Afterward, Naomi might offer to do the dishes in the sink; sincere efforts to repair the relationship are welcome too, so Dad acknowledges this as appropriate. He leaves the room while Naomi does the dishes so as not to escalate a control struggle.

> ☛ **TIP:** Once your child has learned about Consequenceland, she might be tempted to use "repair the relationship" to manipulate the situation. In other words, once she has been given the opportunity to repair the relationship and then chosen not to, she will experience loss of freedom. At that point she

may suddenly change her mind and decide that she'd rather go back and repair the relationship because she doesn't want to go to the thinking chair (or other loss of freedom). However, it is important to follow through with her chosen consequence. If she wants to work on repairing the relationship *after* the loss of freedom, support and recognize this and let her know that you appreciate it.

If Naomi has been used to taking her father's things without permission, then making a different choice is a new behavior for her. It took her a few minutes to comply but she did and Dad can consider that a success. What Dad does not want to do is turn this into a "family tantrum" and expect his daughter to comply without any grumbling the first time. Remember, all new behaviors take time – Naomi might be disgruntled, but when she complies, the consequence ends. A parent needs to know when to disengage and accept a success for what it is and wait for another learning opportunity.

How I Do It

In some families, a consistent approach to behavioral restrictions has not been employed. Therefore the family culture has been one in which the children have learned that if they whine, scream or throw tantrums they can stay in control, since the parents just don't know how to handle it when the volume goes way up. It's easy for parents to overreact in the other direction in an effort to reestablish control. You might find yourself limiting your children's freedom too often in one day. In this case, pause and back up. Reflect on how you can use some creativity and conversation to help your child choose behaviors that do not lead to a restriction in freedom.

One time I was working with a resistant 3-year-old. He had never been taught how to behave in a manner that is expected and appropriate in a social situation. While we were playing, he impulsively head butted me. Yep, that's right, and it hurt! But instead of telling him he had chosen to lose his freedom, and sending him to the thinking chair or quiet room, it was more effective for me to show him that I was hurt and walk him through the process of getting me ice and bandaging my head. In this way, the boy learned a lesson in consequences and responsibility. A negative situation transformed into a positive one. The boy had an opportunity to make amends and be resourceful at the same time.

Anton has a Choice

Anton, age 6, and his step-dad, Mike, are playing ball outside. Anton consistently throws the ball over the back fence when he gets frustrated.

Before you go to Consequenceland, make sure that your child understands the behavioral expectation.

> **Parent:** *"Anton, it is all right to feel frustrated but you need to keep the ball in the backyard. When you throw it over the fence we lose the ball and I have to go get it. If we lose the ball we cannot play anymore."*

Now, move to the first step of Consequenceland: Offer an opportunity to make a better choice.

> **Parent:** *"Anton, you know that you need to keep the ball in the backyard and you are choosing to throw it over the fence. You have one opportunity to make a better choice and keep the ball in the yard."*

Mike goes and retrieves the ball and, again, Anton throws it over the fence.

If necessary, move to the third step in Consequenceland: Loss of freedom. In this case, aside from making Mike go and retrieve the ball, Anton's behavior has not really harmed his relationship with his step-dad; therefore it is appropriate to move directly to loss of freedom here.

Mike tells Anton that he is choosing to lose the opportunity to play ball with his father (a *Level I* consequence).

> **Parent:** *"Anton, you have given away your freedom to play with me. We will go inside now."*
>
> **Anton:** *"No, Mike, I don't want to."*
>
> **Parent:** *"Anton, you are responsible for your choices. You chose to stop playing by throwing the ball over the fence.*

Mike calmly walks Anton inside the house. He goes to the kitchen to get some juice and allows Anton the space to consider the impact of his choices on his opportunity to play.

> ☛ **TIP:** One thing I suggest to parents when they limit a child's freedom is to imagine they are parenting the next-door neighbor. This will allow the parent to take the experience less personally and remain calm. An angry parent cannot implement a consequence effectively because the experience becomes "emotionally charged" and the parent is likely to "climb into the misbehavior instead of modeling appropriate behavior.

Yes, but... *"My kid would be a holy terror once I sent him back inside!"*

OK, sure, but once inside, Anton still has another choice. If he redirects himself and finds an age-appropriate activity, he regains his "freedom" his opportunity to play. With freedom comes the responsibility to use one's mind to engage in play.

If he yells and cries, he will further lose his freedom. Mike will quietly walk Anton to the thinking chair and set the timer for 3 minutes. If Anton stays in the chair and observes his loss of freedom, he can be free in 3 minutes. Anton can hear the timer and he knows what is expected of him. Mike's job is to remain calm and refrain from talking to Anton while he is in the thinking chair – this is key. He must not engage Anton while he is in the thinking chair. There is no discussion – Anton had opportunities to choose a different out-come and these consequences have been made perfectly clear. This way, Mike is re-asserting his place in the hierarchy and showing Anton that his choices calmly result in either freedom (playing) or a loss of freedom (the thinking chair).

There is never any threatening language in Consequenceland, just the truth of the situation, presented in a calm, peaceful way.

When the consequences have been pre-determined, the parent is in the position of guide, mentor, and teacher rather than discipli-narian. Thus, when a child knows what the consequences will be and that he chooses to "go to" a loss of freedom, the control strug-gle between the parent and the child is diminished. With pre-deter-mined, collaborative consequences, the parent can now say to the child, "You have broken a family rule and I am hoping you do not choose Consequenceland because I am enjoying playing this game with you and I want to keep playing with you."

How You Do It
(and how I do it)

When I am in a home teaching proactive parenting, I'll say to a child, "Your family has agreed that if you choose to break the rule, *'we use respectful words,'* then you are choosing the thinking chair consequence. Your parents are your best coaches, they love you, and I am really hoping that we can help you make a better choice so that you do not choose to go there." These sen-tences do two things: First, they engage the child in a process of thinking in order to better manage their behavior, and second, they provide the child a chance to choose an alternate behavior.

Greater Losses of Freedom

More serious misbehaviors warrant greater losses of freedom, of course. Techniques such as the quiet room, like the less restrictive losses of freedom, are designed to re-establish parental control of the situation and assert that children are accountable for their behavioral choices. These are what I call *Level III* consequences, and should be unpleasant but safe. I suggest that these losses of freedom be sufficiently uncomfortable that children will not willingly choose them, yet not physically or emotionally harmful, or frightening, in any way. Each family needs to decide on its own what an appropriate consequence for them is. You might even ask for a consultation with a professional if your child is sufficiently aggressive, or so willing to up the ante that safety is a concern for you.

With children who are willful, stubborn or in poor control of their behaviors, it may come down to the fact that the family has not been "in control" themselves. Or if you have really focused on being mindful, present, calm and consistent, and your child is still non-compliant, they may try to test your patience and see if you can stay that way no matter how far they push you.

It is critical that consequences for these situations are pre-determined. If a parent randomly says "I will take away your Nintendo for a week" one time, and "you are grounded for a week," the next, the child might actually misbehave in order to see what the consequence will be. This creates an escalation in the family, as the child becomes more willful or defiant and the parent gets more out of control.

One of the central purposes of Consequenceland is to shift responsibility for poor behavioral choices to the child – keep this in mind, always.

The mindful parent understands that the child is responsible and accountable for his or her behavior. Collaborating on pre-determined consequences provides the child with the safety of knowing that the parent is now calm and consistent and that the child is expected to behave in accordance with the family values.

Remember the Power of Limbic Overload

In Chapter 8, we reviewed the role of the Caveman and Thinker in managing the limbic system. There are times when children's misbehavior is because of limbic overload. This means that their tempers are hot and they need the skills to calm themselves so they don't climb up to the top of Anger Mountain. As a parent, you can be a source of calm for the child when this escalation begins. By offering new words or behaviors, your children might be able to latch onto a better choice and refrain from choosing a consequence.

In those situations where a child is in this highly charged up state, I usually choose the quiet room technique. These kids usually have worked themselves up because they are no longer "in charge." Here are some pointers to remember:

✦ Most children wish to remain a part of the action. They do not like isolation and find it uncomfortable. When children experience a loss of freedom that isolates them, they understand there is a defined limit to their behavior, and that the family will not accept them willfully breaking the rules and creating disharmony.

✦ Even the most difficult, willful children work hard not to choose this loss of freedom over and over. These kids seek to take control or dominate the family. Once they learn that they are to follow the family norms and will not be allowed to be inappropriately "in-charge," they slowly accept their new position in the family hierarchy.

✦ When faced with the prospect of isolation, a child will likely beg and plead, but it is important for you as a parent not to give in. If you do, you will reinforce his poor choices. But if your child consistently knows that his willful misbehavior will result in a loss of freedom, he will shift his behavior. Breathe through it and stay focused on the goal. *You will need to be calm, peaceful and consistent for the quiet room to work.*

For many children, the quiet room will help them calm their limbic systems and begin to employ thinking strategies to make better choices. But for some other children – those who need to be held or helped to calm down, or compression vests – Consequenceland is not the right option. Consequenceland is for children who are being willfully non-compliant. It is not appropriate for children with neurologically based sensory overload.

How to Implement the Quiet Room Consequence

As we have discussed, it is ideal if children use the opportunity to choose a new behavior. If they don't choose a better behavior or appropriately try to repair the relationship, then a loss of freedom is appropriate. But if your child does not comply with the thinking chair consequence (or similar *Level II* consequences) then he is in effect asking for more discrete limits.

This is where the quiet room comes in. It is a serious *Level III* consequence that is designed to be used as frequently as needed, at first – but your child should not need it for long. Usually 3-5 minutes is enough. You might have to apply it a few times in a row the first time you use the strategy. What you are doing is teaching compliance through peaceful consistency. The fact is that, for a child, accepting you as the top dog may take a bit of repetition. Over time, your kids will be learning from your consistency and limits.

The quiet room functions similarly to the thinking chair, in that your child is restricted to a particular space for a set period of time. It differs in that isolation (the loss of contact with the family) is particularly unpleasant for a child. Isolation says, *"Wait a minute, your behavior is so outside of how we live that you cannot be with us right now."*

NOTE ... A word of caution: If you have a child who cannot man-age his behavior to the degree that several times a day he is experiencing more serious Level II and III consequences (e.g., the thinking chair or quiet room) without any noticeable improvement in his or her behavioral choices, it is likely time to reach out to your pediatrician or a developmen-tal pediatrician in order to have a complete diagnostic evaluation. It is possible that your child may be experiencing more than simple skill defi-cits or willful misbehavior.

Knowledge is Power: Books that Can Help

If you are working with a difficult, willful, non-compli-ant child, you'll want to use every tool at your disposal. Increasing your knowledge to parent requires research, reading, and talking with other parents in order to become more skillful and informed. There are many books that can help you along your way. Here are some I can recommend:

- ✦ *Scream-Free Parenting* by Hal Runkel ("Let the consequences do the screaming.")
- ✦ *Parenting with Love and Logic* by Jim Fay (Why consequences need to be logical, timely, and consistently applied)
- ✦ *Setting Limits with Your Strong Willed Child* by Robert J. MacKenzie (Stopping power struggles before they start)
- ✦ *The Explosive Child* by Dr. Ross Greene (The importance of collaborative decision making with your strong-willed child)

When implementing the quiet room consequence, I'd like you to pay attention to three very important guidelines:

1. Safety First

The quiet room is a safe and secure place, removed from the hubbub of your family's activities. It must contain no objects that could be harmful (upset children can be very creative with ordinary objects!). You may need to clear out a space in order to make sure your child will be safe. The two most common rooms I use are a powder room without a shower or a bathtub, or the laundry room.

If you choose the powder room, all that should be in that room are a toilet and a sink. You must remove all medicines, toiletries, or sharp objects in the cabinet. I prefer that you clean out the entire medicine cabinet, too. Remove any glass shelves that the child might choose to pull down. You want to be prepared for anything from sullen sulks to outright destructive fury. Little ones can do a lot of damage. Make sure that your hot water is not so hot that children could burn themselves. Sit in the room yourself for several minutes with the door both opened and closed and notice what you see and hear. You might observe that you have forgotten to remove an object that could harm your child.

If you choose the laundry room, all that should be in that room are the washer and dryer. You must remove all cleaning solvents and powders to another cabinet in your home. Do not take any risks. If it there is an iron or a solvent in that room, plan on your child gaining access to it and remove it. Do not leave any clothing in there at all.

2. Collaborate With Your Children

Remember, this is a collaborative process, so your child should understand ahead of time that the consequence for certain bad behaviors is the quiet room. Show your children the quiet room. Talk with them about the fact that you prefer they not make a choice to go there, but, ultimately, it is their choice.

3. Age-Appropriate Consequences

The quiet room should be tailored to your child's age and developmental stage. Closed-door isolation is only a solution for children with age appropriate cognitive and developmental skills who are willfully non-complaint and beyond four years of age.

It is not appropriate to isolate a child under four behind a closed door. Children less than four do not have sufficiently developed thinking systems to be sent to closed isolation. Such isolation can be a scary, lonely place where more might be lost than gained. For these children, I recommend increasing time in the thinking chair, or if the child is not complying with the thinking chair, placing it in the quiet room *with the door open*. Most children under four will remain in the chair if the parent stands next to them, quietly and without engaging.

If you require an intervention for a child under four years of age who will not comply when you, 1) increase the timer by three minutes each time he gets up, 2) stand by him in order to encourage compliance, 3) and tell him what he will be able to do once he is up. I encourage you to seek consultation from an Early Childhood Interventionist or your pediatrician. We want to develop skillful, independent, and well-behaved children, not fearful children.

* * *

Now, let's look at a scenario involving the quiet room and see how it all comes together.

Anton Chooses the Quiet Room

Remember Anton, who wouldn't stop throwing his ball over the fence? Let's say he starts yelling and stomping around once Mike, his step-dad, sends him back in the house. In a calm manner, Mike puts Anton in the thinking chair – but Anton keeps getting up and finding things to throw at the wall. Anton knows that the consequences for his behavior have been discussed and planned out. He is aware that he will choose isolation if he does not comply with the thinking chair. Mike gives him one more chance, and then Anton hits him and calls him "stupid!"

It's possible that Anton is actually trying to find out just where the limit is. This is normal, but it is also critical that the parents stay strong and consistent in Consequenceland no matter what. In this situation, Anton will have had the experience of choice, however unpleasant, and this is important for his development.

> **Parent:** *"Anton, you have chosen not to sit in the thinking chair. This means that you will spend five minutes in the thinking room. Please take my hand and we'll go there now."*

Anton is now screaming even louder. Mike touches his shoulder gently as he walks him to isolation in the laundry room. Mike sets the timer for five minutes.

> **Parent:** *"You will remain here for five minutes. At the end of five minutes you can come out and join me in the kitchen to make dinner."*

If Anton yells and cries, that is OK. Mike will ignore that behavior because the goal is for Anton to observe the consequence.

If Anton remains in the space of isolation for five minutes, then the consequence is over. However, if he gets up then Mike tells him he is choosing to have the door shut. Mike turns on the light and closes the door. He remains within earshot but does not talk to or interact with Anton until the timer goes off. It might take several rounds of five minutes before Anton decides to take his consequence. This is a teaching moment for Anton. He is learning that his parents are at the top of the family hierarchy and that he is to comply with his choice to go to the quiet room. After Anton has complied, Mike can be loving and kind; there is no need to hold on to anger or escalate the situation by Mike getting upset too.

It is likely that after isolation Anton may wish to be wrapped tenderly in a blanket or lie on the couch after he is done. The key for Mike is to remain calm. He does not engage Anton with words that will lead to escalation. He does not take Anton's efforts at maintaining control with harsh words or crying personally. He stays calm and recognizes that Anton is really trying to find out if Mike can re-establish control calmly and effectively. And he does.

Bringing it Front of Mind

Later in the evening or the next day when Anton is calm, Mike will review with him the steps that got him to make a choice to go to the quiet room. He will re-assert that it is the purpose of the family to be loving and supportive and that he prefers if Anton makes a better choice next time. In order to reinforce the process of making a better choice, Mike might ask Anton to write a picture story with a beginning, middle and end about keeping the ball in the yard so that next time they can complete their playing outside. If Anton is resistant, Mike can start a story about a dog, cat, elephant or mouse who wanted to do the wrong thing, but chose to do the right thing.

Creativity and bringing better choices front of mind is an important aspect of parenting and setting limits. For the child and family to whom obedience and making good choices is new, it may take several trials of making trying out choices and a little time before the child learns where the limit is. The child will also learn that the parent is going to remain calm and consistent, no matter what comes his or her way. With calm consistency, the misbehaviors of a typical child will decrease as the child's repertoire of better choices evolves.

***

Consequenceland is just one discipline solution. It is designed to provide opportunities for pro-social behavior while establishing limits and re-affirming the line of demarcation when a child exhibits willful non-compliance. If you implement Consequenceland and your child does not appear to develop new skills, begin to respect your guidance, or show an interest in exhibiting behaviors that are consistent with your family norms, then the next step is to seek professional support from your pediatrician or a licensed behavioral health professional. Your family might need more intervention and support. Asking for help is always OK.

Natural, Logical and Self-Chosen Consequences

The key to any system of discipline within a family is fostering strong attachments between the parent (who is guide, teacher, and mentor) and the child (who is developing the skills to be a happy, successful, healthy individual).

Since every child is different, it is important to be open to a variety of approaches to discipline. Several books describe in positive terms why it is so important to use natural, logical and self-chosen (collaborative) consequences. To each author, the specific meanings of these words differ, but the gist is the same. What is most important is not what they mean to the experts, but what they mean to you and how they work in your home. For example, in her book series, *Positive Discipline*, Jane Nelson focuses on solutions instead of punishment. Solutions tend to be more proactive and positive. This is consistent with research that suggests that punishment does not teach pro-social behavior, but solution generation does.

This is really about creative thinking and keeping your eye on the positive. Especially in those early years of parenting, creative thinking about your child's freedom may very well save your sanity.

With new activities, it's helpful to start out managing your child's freedom by making sure they understand that they will get more freedom as they do what is expected.

Here's how my friend Nicole learned how to bring the kids the local superstore without losing her mind:

How Nicole Did It

One day, all hell broke loose at the SuperMart. Her 7-year-old ran up and down the aisles begging for everything in the store, while her 2-year-old yelled over and over for a "blue 'no-cone!" Then, the whole store came to a stop when her 4-year-old jumped out of the cart, ran straight to the automotive section and remained lost for 20 minutes. That night, Nicole called me, sounding absolutely exasperated: "OK, what did you say about that freedom thing? It's not working for me."

"Nicole," I said, "you are an A+ mom, you have three tykes under 7, and we've all been there. Going to the superstore is always going to be a challenge, but you've gotta shop." Then I broke the process down for her:

First, I said, you establish the expectations with your children – *"Kids, we're going to SuperMart. We will: 1) Sit in our spots, 2) Do as Mommy tells you, and 3) Do what is expected."*

Nicole replied that she actually did this before she left the house – she even repeated the instructions in the van on the way.

"Then you manage their freedom with the 20-feet rule," I said.

"Yes, I recall now," Nicole responded. She'd forgotten a technique we'd talked about a while back. Armed with a tape measure and a ticket to Freedomland, here's what Nicole did next time:

> **Nicole:** *"We are going to the SuperMart. You will be good listeners, you will look Mommy in the eyes when I speak, you will do as I tell you. Each of you can earn your freedom when you do what is expected."*

She took out a tape measure and showed the children where 5 feet, 15 feet and 20 feet are – she'd practiced this at home beforehand as well. Here's what she told them:

> **Nicole:** *"We have learned that when we go for a walk, a bike ride or a trip to the store, we observe the 20-feet rule. You start close to Mommy, and when you do what is expected, you get more freedom. If you go past 20 feet, I will yell '20 feet!' and you will sit down wherever you are. If you don't sit down, you will start over at the 5 feet mark."*

How did Nicole do the next time she went shopping with her kids? See for yourself: She started the children out close to her side, the older ones holding on to the cart, the younger ones sitting in the cart. Depending on what was going on in the store and how well behaved the children were being, she gave let them wander to 5 feet, 15 feet and 20 feet. If they behaved inappropriately, she calmly brought them back to 5 feet to start again. Since the 20-foot rule is not punishment, but a skill-development tool, the children never lost the opportunity to earn their freedom.

Now Nicole has a more peaceful experience when she takes the kids out shopping. Sure, it's still a little noisy and silly in her aisle, but everyone is now on the same page. The children know what's expected and Nicole has the tools to keep everyone close by, calm and safe.

Managing Freedom at the Shopping Mall

Here's a quick review of how you can make a trip to the local big box store less chaotic:

1: Establish clear expectations.

2: Assign the children "shopping spots." (inside the cart or holding onto it)

3: Manage their freedom tightly at first.

4: Allow the children more freedom as long as they do as you tell them.

5: Compliment them when they do as expected.

6: Call "20 feet!" if they have been given freedom but roamed too far.

7: Have them start at the 5 feet mark again if they cannot do as expected.

Like all new skills, it takes practice. Try this technique out at home a few times before you use it in public. Remember, if you learn to ride a horse, you start in the small pen before going out on the range. The same is true with teaching your little ones skills.

✔ More Examples of Creativity in Consequenceland

+ When you are working toward proactive solutions for intentional misbehavior, be creative, be loving, be consistent and remain firm. Use common sense and reason to fit the misbehavior and circumstances to the consequence. Here are some other simple examples:

+ When your 3-year-old goes outside near the sidewalk without an adult, take her inside and have her practice telling Mommy she wishes to play outside. Mommy will take her hand and you will play outside together.

+ When your 5-year-old turns on the television in the morning before completing his morning tasks, tell him he will not be allowed to turn on the television at all the rest of the day.

+ When your 7-year-old told you he had no homework, and you learn he had a math page due, tell him you will complete two math practice pages together before dinner.

+ When your 8-year-old hits a ball through the neighbor's window, tell her she will be responsible to earn money for the repairs. You are a family who take responsibility for your actions.

Now, it's likely that you didn't anticipate each of these poor choices, but when you have established a consistent system in your home, based on your Family Mission, Values and Rules, and worked together to make consequences predictable and appropriate, you and your child will be equipped to deal with the problem.

SUMMARY

Parenting is about teaching responsibility and accountability. When you model responsibility and require it of your children, they will grow up to recognize the impact of their behavior on themselves and others and be more accountable for their behavioral choices. This, in a nutshell, is the meaning of *Change You, Change Your Child*.

Your Extraordinary Family Going Forward

❦

It has been my pleasure and my honor to accompany you on this journey. I believe in The Family Coach Method and I believe in your power as a parent to create Your Extraordinary Family in collaboration with your children. My role has been to offer you tools and encouragement for the road ahead. I sincerely hope your journey will lead you to a higher functioning, more joyful family.

Please don't hesitate to let me know how you are doing; I really want to know. If you have any questions, concerns or comments, you can reach me online at www.lynnekenney.com. Tell me what is working for you and send me your own "How I Do It's." I'll post the best ones on my website. As I said in my Introduction, we're in this together. The Family Coach Method exists to evolve and grow, and you are a vital part of that growth.

Acknowledgments

✿

When Nancy Goldman asked me about 18 months ago, "How is your book coming along," she spring-boarded me to action, for which I will always be grateful. My husband Rick provided me the garden in which to nourish the tales within. Dr. Ron Fischler and our colleagues at North Scottsdale Pediatrics gave me the finest practice imaginable in which to bring The Family Coach Method alive. Without you, this book would still be an idea. Thank you deeply.

My editors at St. Lynn's Press, Cathy Dees and Abby Dees, are master-crafters of the "author's voice." Working with you, as I tell my husband, was one of my most memorable life experiences. You lived The Family Coach concept of "We lift one another up." Paul Kelly, my publisher: you gambled and I thank you.

Tracy McCormick, you are the diamond who started it all; I will never forget your selfless contributions. Brienne Hollingsworth, you are and will always remain an inspiration. Diana Vigil, you are the intelligent mind in this book; seek and you will find, speak and you will grow. All of you show that colleagues can work on the positive side of relationships. It has been a joy. Thank you.

The acknowledgments for this book start way back in the 1970's when I had the closest friends a teenager could ask for. I still admire these women today: Maureen Martin, Juli Missimer and Jennifer Wood. Vanessa Fishman, Elizabeth Dean, and Justine Gilman, EdD, are wonderful influences of reflection.

Alex Brousseau, Lisa Voss, Jeanne Fletcher, Lila Baltman, Nicki MacDonald, The McWilliams Family, The McFischer Family, The Davis Family, The Kenney Family, The Trudo Family, The Joren Family, The McSwain Family, Amy Bubier, Susan Link, Dr. Tom Merrill, and Julie Skakoon: you create our memories past and present.

Michele Borba, EdD, Michelle LaRowe, Maria Bailey, Bradi Nathan, Megan Calhoun, Bobbie Sandoz Merrill, MSW, and Kathy Ireland: your thoughts, words and talent change lives.

My academic mentors are many. A few to whom I owe warm thanks include: John Callaghan, PhD, Ron Schouten, MD, Bernard Pipkin, PhD, Allen Brown, PhD, Richard Cone, EdD, Mary Murray, Annette Brodsky, PhD, Alfredo Saavedra, John Moran, PhD, Karen Saywitz, PhD, Kathy Gilbride, PhD, Jeff Seigel, MD, Raun Melmed, MD, Kathi Borden, PhD, Ed Shafranske, PhD, Cheryl Saunders, and Karen van der Veer, NMD.

Barrie Gillies, you make me laugh. Tracy Kornet, thank you for the break into TV; you are elegant. Paul Rosengard and SPARK PE, you save lives. To the members of the International Nanny Association and The National Head Start Association, thank you for making a difference in the lives of children.

Dr. Dana-Marie Thomas, Jeff Quinn, Dana Herzberg, Nicole Jewell, Anita Werner, Linda Levin, Beth Callahan, Kathy Greenberg, Lori Schulman, Amanda Veith, Katrina Goldberg, Cynthia Malinski, Dianne and Marty Lundy, David and Allison Weinstock, Lori Black, Katie Greene, Kris Greene, Vickie Garcia, The Moms of NCPG and The Moms of Wildfire: you give so much to the families you love, educate and care for. I thank you for your advice, support and contributions.

Over the years I have had the opportunity to work with the most amazing families; bright, caring, intelligent parents who want the best for their children. Children who are creative, compassionate and committed to learning. Thank you all – warmly – for your honesty, courage and hard work.

About the Author

Lynne Kenney, Psy.D. is a mom and a practicing pediatric psychologist in Scottsdale, AZ. She has advanced fellowship training in forensic psychology and developmental pediatric psychology from Massachusetts General Hospital/Harvard Medical School and UCLA Medical School.

Dr. Kenney is a consultant to The International Nanny Association and The National Head Start Association, and was NHSA's 2007 National Ambassador. As an "expert mom" she has been featured in Parents, Working Mother, and Success magazines. Her parenting advice and tips can also be found on Twittermoms and BlogTalk Radio (The Family Coach Show) – and in the DVD's and other programming content that she produces for the BabyFirst TV channel.

She lives in Scottsdale with her husband and two daughters.

Dr. Kenney can be contacted at *www.lynnekenney.com*.